CLXI Inner Mountain Thoughts

A Journey to Self-Discovery

Byron (Be Positive) Gaskins

BALBOA.
PRESS

A DIVISION OF HAY HOUSE

Balboa Press books may be ordered through booksellers or by contacting:

Balboa Press
A Division of Hay House
1663 Liberty Drive
Bloomington, IN 47403
www.balboapress.com
1 (877) 407-4847

Print information available on the last page.

ISBN: 978-1-9822-1628-3 (sc)
ISBN: 978-1-9822-1629-0 (e)

Balboa Press rev. date: 05/09/2019

CONTENTS

NOTES

Preface

I would like to tell you a little bit of how this book came to be as you begin reading it. *The Power of Positive Thinking* by Dr. Norman Vincent Peale was one of the first books my mother, Electa Mae Wilson gave me when I could read and being positive is my mantra. Since my early teen years, I have sought and found spiritual openings that lead to an expanded recognition of the grander part that I am.

By age 16 I felt spiritually starved and left the Baptist church after hearing about the death of Jesus with no new information. Shortly after that Easter Sunday I found myself taking A *Lessons in Truth* course at the local Unity Church in Springfield, Ohio. This course was my springboard. Through it I learned how to read the Bible more holistically. Encouraged by my mother, I began Inner Peace Movement studies, learning of my gifts and angels, experiencing energy fields, thought transference and mind over matter techniques. During my college years I studied I Ching and Scientology. The later helped tremendously in college studies. Even now I use the techniques for the benefit of myself and others. I became involved again in the traditional church during the late 80s and 90s, becoming a deacon and completing Baptist Theological Seminary certification. This led to studies in Judaism, Kabbalism, Tibetan rites and other sacred sciences. All of this marvelous education laid the foundation for even greater gifts I received from working with the healers and ministers of the Healing Hearts Center in Bettendorf, Iowa. Along with learning of various healing modalities and establishing some very deep friendships I absorbed Spring Forest Qi Gong from Master Chunyi Lin. It was during these years I returned to my New Thought Ancient Wisdom roots as a member of the Unity

Church of Christianity in Moline, IL., filling my free time studying *A Course in Miracles* and Joel Goldsmith's *Infinite Way* writings. In 2005 my mother invited me to attend my first Revelations Conference sponsored by Agape International Spiritual Center in Los Angeles. I returned from that conference deeply feeling the words 'I am only here for God.' It was the beginning of a renewed personal endeavor to expand in internal ways. Up till then I had been wading in the tidewaters of sincere soulful evolution. This personal turning point propelled me to obtain my metaphysical minister's certification in 2009.

While attending a minister's conference at Agape in 2011, I was overtaken each day with a need to journal what my heart heard during meditations and conversations and even during sleep. It was during this time that *Thoughts from the Inner Mountains* began building. Each day brought new revelations and insights. They have not stopped. My close circle of friends, family therapist, qigong and other spiritual health practitioners, all wealthy ministers in their own right, encouraged me. They coached me into deeper soul expanding practices enabling me to handle my own baggage. Their work helped me carve pathways that led to bigger love experiences and gave me the surefootedness I would need as Spirit channeled such powerful insights through me.

Some of the 'thoughts' came from circumstances that caught my attention while others came from nature and God knows where. The blessing for me is to catch a glimpse of how the Infinite Spirit lifts us to see differently and often more clear. This walk has allowed me to look at the underbelly and backside of a situation and to not be afraid of the grit and grind of honest spiritual work.

I believe the Divine intent of these writings is to reinvigorate our response to Spirit's call of living a serenely magnificent life.

I was unsure how to present these words of grace and truth because the style and format were unfamiliar to me. Yet is was resolved by a conversation with Dr. Michael Beckwith without me even telling him my dilemma. He encouraged me to read the works of Dr. Howard Thurman and of course I did. After a few weeks, I got it. Dr. Thurman's revered works are contemplative and in a personalized style not laden with much doctrine or must dos, thus the style and format of Inner Mountains.

I offer you the reader these writings for enjoyment, inspiration, humor, reflection and reverence. They are signposts, stories and teaching/learning points gifted from an Eternal Breath that continues to move my soul as I navigate the Inner Mountains.

Always

Reverend B+...

NOTES

THOUGHT #1

Perspective

We are always taller than we seem. We may get depressed looking at other people's circumstances, or our perceived problems and situations, yet remember we are always taller than them. Those situations may even seem insurmountable and above our shoulders or beyond reach. Yet never forget there is more to us than the level of our eyes and what we see.

Dare to enlarge your vision by keeping the added measure of your stature in perspective. Looking back, we see by divine fortune we are here. I invite my family, friends and folks I used to consider my enemies to embark on this fresh palette of goodness. In a more relaxed, confident manner, let us once again be open to the real power bending the iron rod of our seeming indifferences. Let the Master Harmonizer weave that precarious communication we need to have with someone even if it is with ourselves. Let our vision be on an upward level like Martin Luther King Jr. who dreamed a dream for a society much larger than his own congregation. We are always taller than we seem. We have power, a right and a responsibility to leap tall buildings consistent with our consciousness. This is what we *want*.

Surely the branch would suffice it a good thing to be reconciled with the vine so it can realize what it knows deeply. That it is taller than the level of its current or previous separate version of itself. Surely, we have built a miracle or mess of our lives thus far (as we see it) yet remember we are always taller than the level at which we see.

In the words of Professor Klump say," Yes I can" 20 times before you fall into sleepsville.

THOUGHT #2

Heart Thoughts

What do we know of the heart's unspoken promises to itself? Do we hear them? Will we honor and embrace them? Nurture them? And cherish them as they grow?

THOUGHT #3

Contemplate This

What do we pray for once the storm is over?

THOUGHT #4

Knowledge

Mere knowledge of Supreme Intelligence or that contained in Holy writings is eclipsed by the transcendent transforming experience of communing with the Divine. Gandhi demonstrated this.

THOUGHT #5

Life Connection

Today we celebrate the life that was lived as Loren Crownover at the River House in Moline, IL. If you ever spoke with Loren you knew you were in for a lively and thought-provoking conversation with a lot of love. To honor all life is to know it as our own.

"ALL THINGS ARE CONNECTED. WHATEVER BEFALLS THE EARTH BEFALLS THE SONS OF THE EARTH. MAN DID NOT WEAVE THE WEB OF LIFE. HE IS MERELY A STRAND IN IT. SO, WHATEVER HE DOES TO THE WEB, HE DOES TO HIMSELF." -CHIEF SEATTLE, 1854

THOUGHT #6

Intercommunicating by Design

I had a new thought on relationships while reviewing a technical manual on inflatable boats. The main float channels can be inflated singularly or simultaneously when the valves are in a certain setting. Intercommunicating is when the valves are set so that the air chambers are open to each other. This made me think of how both parties in a relationship of any kind must be completely open in order to be filled or 'inspired' for a common purpose. In this setting either one can be 'filled' and positively impact the other party and the relationship as a whole. The key here is that both can experience an infilling of Dynamic Presence because they are intercommunicating.

THOUGHT #7

Solving Problems

It has been said that signs and miracles follow advances in spiritual consciousness. St. Paul was right when he said, *flesh and bone cannot inherit the kingdom of God.* For that Kingdom is a place of supreme consciousness not under the confines or dictates of this third dimensional state of existence. Jesus said the Kingdom was here and now; *nearer than hand and foot.* Symbolically, he spoke of something we cannot grasp nor completely understand from third dimension thinking or beliefs. Signs and miracles always occur outside time–space reality. They are expressed through those available (even momentarily) to Divine Creative Energy. Consider looking at the surface of a chess board versus looking at it from beneath. We cannot begin to make better choices in our lives until we desire more understanding through holy contemplation. Once we gain that higher perspective, then we take a step up on the ladder and can more appropriately address what was amiss before we knew better.

David the Psalmist said *surely goodness and mercy will follow me all the days of my life.* Now is the time. Do you know where your thoughts are playing?

THOUGHT #8

Communion

We can experience communion with the Divine when we get out of the circle of time and get into the circle of love. Rumi spoke of this in one of his many love poems about the Divine. Our contemporary culture and personal learning often decry this seeming abandonment of structures and paradigms. Yet we are assured by the many that have traveled this route, travailed that awesome course and trampled the opposing thoughts and contradictory actions. For as many laws, codicils, rituals, doctrines and heaven help us 'dogmas', there are multitudes more personal stories of revelatory trysts with the Divine.

Take time to find out how the great Spirit of Life speaks to you. There you will find the most sacred; the most pleasurable; and the most satisfying. Rest in peace and labor not in vain.

THOUGHT #9

The Bounty of Our Souls

Our True Being birthed of God always remains unscathed by the temporal. Only the temporal mind can entertain the things of the temporal.

Nothing exists without the Infinite and yet the Finite continues to struggle with its True Birthright. Infinite Life makes all possible even when shadows fall. Therefore, know Peace this day.

THOUGHT #10

Freedom

The freest country is the one you think and feel with. Yes, that's right, your 'heartmind'. The question unfurls like a big red flag, who is holding you back from excellence? Now, what happens when you run out of other people to blame? Relax, take a step this minute to expand your 'liberation consciousness'. Go down the stairs backwards. You know you are FREE to do that even if your brain asks 'why are you doing this?' Your NEW RESPONSE: 'Cause I CAN, I am Free. I am in my free country!'

THOUGHT #11

Stretch Your Wings and Fly

Sometimes it feels good to dwell in the atmosphere of the Ostrich. To feel the splendid warmth of the earth and air. There is a level of certainty and comfort found there. Yet, that bird cannot fly. The dream of your soul requires you to elevate, so take note of how your heart feels and start stretching those wings.

THOUGHT #12

Contemplate a New Thought

Often, we are tempted to wear the mantle of humanity so tightly wrapped in our belief systems that we can be just a hair's breadth from spontaneous combustion. Nonetheless we are also taught by the great contemporary Master and Teacher to take no thought... In other words, we are to forsake impermanence and trivial lower thoughts. It is the Invisible that gives life to the visible. Ask any artist, architect, or creator. Both the malady and the miracle occur on the planes within. Our favorite radio station is invisible to us yet it's our favorite for some reason. We are attuned to it. Is it the news, or the music? Since our life is anchored in the eternal rhythmic heartbeat, can we feel that melody, that spiritual salsa dissolving our fear, anger, inner resistance, or stubborn thought? Spit out the human concept and contemplate a new thought of relative divinity. Are we of the earth or spiritually conceived? As one famous fellow put it... Choose this day whom you will follow.

THOUGHT #13

Gratitude

Being on fire with gratitude can be likened to a wayward, excited child running loose in the marketplace. It pulls at the shelves of complacency and smiles at consternation. It rubs grease on the curtains of time while placing seemingly priceless wagers on big things. It places its feelings above the rim of the cup and spills laughter everywhere. Gratitude knows it is magnetic and draws the attention of the Universe! Has anybody seen this child?

THOUGHT #14

Lucky Number 11

Numerologically speaking 3.31.13 adds up to 11. On this resurrection day, let us celebrate living life anew, having in some manner experienced a stone or two being rolled away. Yet now we are faced with a curious dilemma. We have returned to an empty tomb. One that imprisoned us, kept us bound in heart and mind. It is empty now because we asked, searched and knocked for a promise, for relief, for more. Symbolically, that which plagued us was exchanged for that which saved us.

Yet who is freed and what do we look like? Now that burdens are left by the riverside; baggage gone or reframed we breathe a little lighter. The consequence of the early stages of spiritual liberation is identity crisis. We are not who was in the tomb of undesired circumstances. Our confusion hinges on which of the three kings we are letting govern our perception. If we are at the tomb looking for our mortal incomplete ego self it is not there. If we are seeking a scripted intellectual persona, then we are still facing an empty tomb and will feel it in our gut. That's the flaw of observing the second king. Now the third king brings us to a level of trusting in the Divine to show us a new image of ourselves. That image is not static so we must always be in a state of letting go and allowing for spiritual re-formation. Key point here is that the resurrected Self is not necessarily one we are going to even recognize. Our mortal eyes and imperfect vision won't see the new us. That means a lot of changes. The resurrected Self is new territory. We are equipped with new powers and knowledge to be comprehended. This new image of us is in the likeness of that which creates constantly. Go find yourself in Life all around you.

THOUGHT #15

Have an Inspired Vision

It's a good measure of inspired understanding from the writer of '... without vision the people perish.' The uninspired with loose-knit understanding will agonize over every seeming defeat and will focus only on the four fingers in front of their face of their life appearing as real. Next, we find the prayerful soul learned and heaped in religious teachings and some spiritual illumination crying out 'Let me recognize the problem so it can be solved.' Now as those echoes turn to sweet butter we find a most peaceful soul with an understanding of 'I am one with the Father' stating humbly yet profoundly, 'Let me recognize my problems have been solved.' Why may you ask? Because the one that understands the phrase 'my life is hid in thee...,' sees beyond the four fingers. They have a vision of living a fulfilled life.

THOUGHT #16

Belief

Belief is very powerful. Then comes the state of Knowingness. Experience is the transformational emissary between them.

THOUGHT #17

Truth

"Truth is freestanding. Its credibility does not depend on anything external. Its authority comes from the reality of that which it is. Which is purely subjective and experiential."

– Dr. David R. Hawkins

Water by description does not make it what it is. Truth is, it just is.

THOUGHT #18

Sane Insanity

'Falling in love is kind of like being considered out of one's mind. Except in the latter case one does not have an excuse nor have to have an explanation.'

– Coz Ruthles

THOUGHT #19

Our Role

Quantum physics has taught us much about our spiritual evolution. It has revealed that each of us plays a larger part in the lives of others than previously considered. Although, out of innocence and ignorance we sometimes tryout for other roles or accept those bestowed on us. Hence, we go making a mess of the scene, maybe even the whole act, all before intermission. Thank Omnigod for intermission! Then when we arrive at a different place, we laugh about the whole thing and forgive ourselves!

THOUGHT #20

Benefit of the Cup

Before any judgment to cast the first stone, let us seek an understanding not of our own. Let us seek the benefit of the cup! The cup of understanding that is formed as we allow ourselves to shift through at least 360 degrees of perspectives. Having done so we may arrive at an opinion that just might hold water. The cup! Continual efforts of this nature will move us towards a place of no judgment and eventually to a place of happiness rather than of rightness. A place where we begin to value our own internal pleasantness so much that we will not allow anything to disturb it. It is from this internal sacred pivot point that unconditional love grows.

THOUGHT #21

Choices

"The reality is that choices that support our long-term fulfillment aren't always fun. They aren't the easiest or sexiest choices to make. But making choices with our future in mind is vital if we want to make our vision for our lives a reality...when we make choices that are in direct conflict with our dreams, we rob ourselves of the future we desire."

– Debbie Ford

The goal for our heart should be to live as true to its desires and choices as possible in all situations.

THOUGHT #22

4 Questions from Vernon Howard

"How would you feel if you had no fear? Feel like that.

How would you behave towards other people if you realized their powerlessness to hurt you? Behave like that.

How would you react to misfortune if you saw its inability to bother you? React like that.

How would you think towards yourself if you knew you were really all right? Think like that."

Our objective then, is to think clearly about our response to all situations and be aware that our reactions are how we believe.

THOUGHT #23

Reality

After years of teachings, preaching and reading, one thing lingers. This one voluntary thread that has stood out as a lifeline as I weave and swing through this dimension called 'reality.' It is so profound everyone who reads it will get it. It will help in defining prayer work; assist the intellectual, clarify issues at hand and purify the conveyance of information. This thread has been extremely helpful for developing perspectives that lead to purer forms of knowledge. This tool is:

BLESS EACH SITUATION AS IT IS. NO ADJECTIVES NO MODIFIERS AND NO EXAGGERATION.

THOUGHT #24

Be the Cause!

OK slow your roll... if just momentarily take pause from the daily grind.

The word, "because," slow it down there, be... cause means Be Cause. Be the Cause. Re-present God on earth right now. Such that all who seek the light will find it in you. Be Cause.

THOUGHT #25

Ever-Presence

What we find most intriguing about the ego is its ability to keep us in a pleading, clinging, unfulfilled, and unhappy paradigm.

For instance, when a couple goes to break up, one or both of the egos want everything. The ego feels justified to have a major share of the material assets because its feelings are hurting and it has invested so much time.

What the ego will try not to reveal is the cooperative and loving spirit of the Ever-Present Self. The Ever-Present Self knows only love, whose actions are focused on giving and living. Not dicing and sacrificing.

The Ever-Present Self will seek the perfect outcome not based on what or who is wrong or right.

The feelings can only be hurt if ego is clinging to something that happened 'so five minutes ago'. We should take some time to search our mind for any hurt feelings. Once we locate a feeling of hurt, ask ourselves when did that occur? Did it just happen in the PAST five seconds? If so then we have an excellent opportunity to try a holistic alternative with no side effects.

If something has occurred in our past still containing a charge (draws strong emotion) then we acknowledge the ego has created a bill for us. A debt that comes with INTEREST. Now notice that the debt (hurt feeling) has increased because the original situation that may have 'caused' those feelings is no longer a present activity.

Herein lies the quandary. The past cannot be undone and yet the ego will not let us off the hook nor the person, place or thing we feel wronged us. It won't let us off the hook of feeling hurt and it won't let go from our subconscious thinking processes without intervention. This introduces the concept of 'sacrifice'. Here again the ego asks us to give up something furthering our degree of involvement with a noncurrent event and our unhappiness now with ourselves multiplies and resentment increases. It has us feeling that some person, place or thing got the best of us and to have some peace of mind we have to 'lose'. Summarily this keeps us in a cycle of unhappiness until we recognize Ever-Presence.

THOUGHT #26

New Perspective

In the wake behind accepting an ego alternative, we enter a remorseful period. Many kick themselves for not choosing higher ideals after reflecting on their decisions. Yet since Infinite Love abides, hope remains. Consequently, space for a new perspective is born, sponsored in part by our willingness to choose again. Remember judgment, even of ourselves takes us further away from our Holy Vibration.

THOUGHT #27

Creativity

The world we think we know by sight has always been challenged both by science and by spiritual theorists, philosophers and avatars. The latter group includes the likes of Lao Tzu, Yogananda, The Buddha, Gandhi, and Jesus. There are more that have been major players in the revelation of new perspectives.

Whole societies have been uplifted because of their contemplative work. Following is an example of simple comparative examination that supports the value of evolutionary thought research. Take the Bible story of Job. The traditional approach is that Job's faith was tested. However, hidden within the third chapter of that Bible book, we discover that Job was using the power of creativity fearfully looking for something to go wrong. Obviously, Job did not understand at least two things. First, that he had innate creative ability. The defining nature of Source or God is the desire and ability to create. We are made in the image and likeness of It. Secondly, as quantum physicists, Thomas Edison and others have scientifically proven, the energies of fear or love are 'attractor factors' that bring circumstances into our lives every day. Thanks to Job (an Old Testament story), we can see how what we focus on can become a reality. Centuries later (in the New Testament), Jesus said it another way that according to your heartfelt belief it will be done. Jesus was explaining the power of creativity and the law of attraction as amplified in the phrase 'as a man thinks in his heart so is he.'

What will you be creating and experiencing today?

THOUGHT #28

Truth

Truth will correct all errors in my mind (*A Course in Miracles* Lesson #107). We know this at the deepest level of who we are. Lao-tzu knew this too. Thanks to Galileo and Columbus for demonstrating how errors in thinking are dealt with by the collective mind. It takes internal commitment to an ideal, an acceptance of that which is not seen but felt as it is given from Purity. This is what is meant by the phrase Truth is experiential. In the 1500s, Galileo received the inspiration to affirm that the sun was the center of our planetary system, not the earth. This was a major departure from accepted European belief. Erroneously, that new paradigm was fought against with great fervor by religion, so much that Galileo was pressured to recant the Truth that was granted him. Christopher Columbus's belief of a round world helped correct another error in belief. Now when we look at what comes to us via space scopes and we think WOW, is this what Galileo saw? Even our individual worlds hold much wonder and beauty when we let Truth correct errors in our minds.

THOUGHT #29

Rules of the Road

In life never pick up a hitchhiker unless they are going your way or express intent to go where you are headed. Conversely, for the hitchhiker, not everyone who asks if you need a ride should be giving you one. On the surface these tenets may seem very elementary yet in terms of relationships these guides can be helpful.

Some of us are headed in a specific direction and many times we pick up people in life that have other stops to make that dissipate our original focus. All this is OK if we are willing to forego our agendas. If it bothers us we may be suffering from taxi-itis. Where our lives become running errands with our partners till at some point we drop it or stop it. Now the hitchhikers, those waiting for a ride may have a reason for not moving further along, perhaps unsure of a life direction or maybe even hoping someone comes along that will make a nice life for them or offer some complimentary resources they feel they need. Now the hitchhiker should be wary about forming a relationship with someone who seems more focused on picking up someone to travel with than about where they are headed. The truth is both have baggage. So, when you give to or help others, do it without attachment, expectation of results or being appreciated or recognized. Don't get upset if you get put out at the next stop or surprised if the hitchhiker doesn't appreciate the ride.

THOUGHT #30

Remember

When appearances of disease, lack, hatred and sadness or whatever else disturbs your peace remember this: It is the grind that sharpens the axe that fells the tree that builds the house that love abides in.

THOUGHT #31

How It Works

"In Creation it appears God sleeps in the minerals, dreams in the flowers, awakens in the animals and in man knows that It is awake"

– Paramahansa Yogananda

We live expressly as the Divine becomes conscious of Itself and we do too.

THOUGHT #32

I Surrender Myself to God

The central element in communion with God is the act of self-surrender. The symbol of my prayer this day is the open heart. It is most natural for me to think of prayer in terms of the open hand. My needs are so great and often so desperate that there seems to be naught besides my own urgency. I must open my heart to God. This will include my own deep urgencies and all the warp and woof of my desiring. These things, deep within, I must trust with the full awareness that more important even than self-realization is the true glorifying of God. Somehow, I must make God central to me and in me, over and above the use to which I wish or need to put *Its* Energy and *Its* power.

I surrender myself to God without any conditions or reservations. I shall not bargain with God. I shall not make my surrender piecemeal but shall lay bare the very center of me, that all of my very being shall be charged with the creative energy of God. Little by little, or vast area by vast area, my life must be transmuted in the life of God. As this happens, I come into the meaning of true freedom and the burdens that I seemed unable to bear are floated in the current of the life and love of God. From Howard Thurman's *Meditations of the Heart*

It is with releasing the idea of a separate self from Source that we can experience something higher and more meaningful to live by and as.

THOUGHT #33

Calling

I was out with my grandchildren the other day and observed certain aspects of their behavior that led me to conclude what each might be when they proverbially 'grow up'. Their answers were a little different than my guesses. Of course, the deeper question to myself was are they aware of their Calling. Only time will tell. Of course, I don't have to be right about what they will do in life. Although I would venture to say that very few of us at age 2 or three have zeroed in on what we want to be. Even into our twenties and later, we are trying to figure out who we are, how we fit, and what is in this thing called life for me. In reading many bios one thing comes to certain the job, the position... The CALLING happened when they were least expecting yet 'their bags were packed'. I found myself answering the deeper question this way: I did not intentionally shape my Calling. Rather my life experiences did the shaping so when it happened my bags were packed. I just found out about it as it unfolded.

THOUGHT #34

Our Response to the Calling

I have not intentionally shaped my calling. Rather Life has shaped it. At backward glance all the stuttering, counseling, and the moments of feeling left out, were actually defining moments moving me towards fulfillment of the Calling. Along the way I picked up such tools as meditation. So, I offer this insight as lovingly as I can on this day of rebirth, that if your present and past life seems like a mess, it probably is and that's OK. Because you have just been packing to take the journey your Life has called you to. Relax, the Omniverse has the map just let go! Remember to let go of the baggage!

THOUGHT #35

Selective Hearing

Only your misperceptions stand in your way..." Many are called but few are chosen" should be, "All are called but few choose to listen." Therefore, they do not choose right...Right minds can do this now, and they will find rest unto their souls. Says *A Course in Miracles*.

To be soul deaf is being resistant to a better feeling life. Only hearing with your ears when there is so much that is inaudible is selective hearing.

THOUGHT #36

Accept a New Perspective

We are never aware of more than we can accept. This is the great blindness of our own choosing. Often, we will forsake the promising feeling of a new perspective only to keep self-frustration nursing us in our idle hours. Many a great discovery lay dormant for years like the bamboo plant, then given the right yearning and inquisitiveness it grows swiftly beyond anticipation. From the Wright brothers' flying machine to the Hubble Space scope took barely one hundred earth years. The laws of physics and aerodynamics were the same two thousand years ago yet the contemplation of flight was literally left to the birds and angels. What is in our hearts that we have been nursing? Is it something we simply need to have a magnificent acceptance of?

THOUGHT #37

Losing Craziness

I was sane. Then went insane. And that's a good thing. I had to lose my mind to find IT... so now that I am HERE....

Stay in Infinity...

Oh, Source of Lights I do cherish thee.

My fragile nature, my seeds deep inside...

Thou have liberated me

And caused my wayward

horses to collide.

In time, I stand still to let smokeless clouds settle

And meddle not with the dawn,

For you Source – Oh Light of

Lights, have never left me.

I am always in your Mind

As a sweet thought, a significant construct of your Love and Beauty.

My gaze is your Gaze, my walk is your

Walk.

The touch is a surreal interface directly

from the Cosmos. A cool fire that delivers

Grace from beyond... transforming all with

IT's Presence.

I love thee. I love this place.

I love the stay in Infinity.

THOUGHT #38

Sadness

Sadness is a wonderful journey when hope shows up. The kind of hope not built on ecstasy – physical or in tablet form.

Hope represents what is extruded from memory of previous successes, even if those come from the cling-clang in the recesses of our minds.

We treasure hope as a god to deliver us from sadness when in fact many would choose to stay there a little longer.

Staying in sadness can be an attractor for more of the same. Ask anyone who seems to carry that trait.

Yet sadness lives with us like almost too ripe fruit. One more day and it will surely stink up the place.

Embrace sadness, feel it and then face it with a watchful guard upon the heart. For if it takes up residence there, it can tear you apart.

THOUGHT #39

Joy Puppies

We toy with joy like our neighbor's new pup. We offer to feed it treats, scraps and even tease it a little to hear its yelp. All the while thinking I am not taking care of such a creature. I don't have the room or time to train it.

We entertain thoughts of having joy yet can't seem to commit to the care and feeding of it. We would rather someone else raise it, then we can play with it occasionally till our hearts feel good. Following this we withdraw to our private life where fear, doubt, and worry nips at our heels from room to room. Alas we pause and confess if I only had joy right now everything would be blessed.

THOUGHT #40

More Joy Puppies

We soon find that letting someone else raise our joy becomes an issue of dependency, where we start living off other's energy and their life so much that we can lose sight of what really makes our joy. Suppose we start today to list what really turns us upward and build on that. At least two things will start happening in our lives: We will feel our power coming back and we experience more the 'joy' pup growing in our heart!

THOUGHT #41

Flow

"When we dedicate our life to right seeing, right being, time will stop. We will drop the need to live in the past or project into the future. The eternal moment, just as it is, will reveal its perfection to us, and we will merge our consciousness into the One Perfection."

- Dr. Michael Bernard Beckwith

It says we don't have to figure it all out but we do have to exhale to get in step with the Flow.

THOUGHT #42

Faithing

The most we could ever subscribe to regarding faith is that of the idea it carries and promotes. It becomes the active component in launching ahead. It moves us ever onward, towards the unseen dream, objective or circumstance. What we believe we receive. Faithing is an active psychic component, not a static noun.

THOUGHT #43

Freedom from Baggage

Having said the benediction, we lay aside our differences for the last time. Peace becomes us as its big sister Love watches on. We know the rest of our days will be oh, so very well! You see Love creates a safe place in our hearts where others can abide without contempt or judgment. When they feel our sincerity, all resistance passes from us and them also. The road behind us exists no more. We will not use it to travel forward so we let it go. This is attested to by the long, deep looks we fearlessly take through each other's eyes. We have liberated ourselves from the need to be right and renewed friendships begin. For our freedom is contingent on setting others free from the maladies of the human persona. Be they guilt, shame, feelings of not enoughness or whatever. We find in retrospect their bondage was our baggage. But now we are free!

THOUGHT #44

Beauty Arises

As Beauty arises in us, It sees Itself everywhere through our eyes and senses. It quickly and with certainty fastens Itself to the rays of the morning sun so all can benefit throughout the day. So as the day comes and goes when people look at you rather oddly just remember they are seeing the Beauty that shines as You!

THOUGHT #45

The Enclosed Lamp

There are some of us who listen to a personal record of circumstance, insult and regret for so long that we begin to believe it is real. We believe that somehow it is our destiny, our cross and somehow holy. Then we arrive at a mid-spring morning and admit that we cannot live another moment like this. We, from our hearts desire change. Life will see that it happens. We expose ourselves to the True Flame of Love and Grace Beyond Beauty and are willing to be touched by It. We will allow the Open Flame to singe our soul. Leaving a print upon our heart, and inexplicable radiance. Those preferring to live within the confines of self-believed circumstances are refusing the joyous transformational luminosity of the Open True Flame and entertaining themselves as moths by an old post lamp. The enclosed lamp offers little transformational value for the Light cannot touch them.

THOUGHT #46

A New Original Thought

There is a great urgency brewing amidst the angst already flooding our society today. It is a subtle survival mechanism of the original Divine Ideal that we come from. That urgency is to reclaim our minds. Yes, this urgency comes at the end of the rope scenario with little things like bills unpaid, emotions unsettled, intentions and wishes seemingly washed out like old faded dishcloths. The reason for this compelling evolutionary action towards new thought paradigms is to live a fuller expression of life sooner rather than later. We take back the structures and abilities of our minds to use in forming Good tomorrows and even the next five seconds. Starting with remembering and centering on this Seed thought'... made in the image and likeness of....'

THOUGHT #47

Nonpontification

From *Tales of the Hasidim* by Martin Buber, a tale is told of Rabbi David of Lelov. The Rabbi observed a man praying and saying the name of God after every verse. After inquiry it was learned the man had mistaken the two dots one above the other as each the tiny letter Yud or Yod. Since the name of God is sometimes abbreviated in the form of two Yuds, he thought that is what he saw at the end of each verse. The Rabbi of Lelov instructed the man: "Wherever you find two Jews [Yuds] side by side and on par, there is the name of God. But whenever it looks to you as if one Jew [Yud] were standing above the other, then they are not Jews [Yuds] and it is not the name of God.

God/Love is hard to be found when one puts oneself above another. Rabbi David uses this moment not to humiliate the man with a lesson in reading so much as to teach a transcendent message. Demonstrating how to stand side by side with someone and come from a place of God/Love. This story teaches us of nonpontification. Let us note how we position ourselves such that the name of God or Goodness will be present in our communion with one another.

Where two or more are gathered the I AM is Present.

THOUGHT #48

Prayer for Another

From time to time many of us are asked to pray for another. Do we ever stop to ask what shall I pray for about this individual? If one stays in that vein of thought more may be accomplished than if we immediately begin asking God to fix something. The attitude of 'what shall I pray for' empties us of the quick reactive thought and allows for fresh inspiration of best how to commune with That Which is All. It is beneficial to link our minds to Source so we remove the 'mote' in our eyes of fault be it sickness, poverty or bad attitude, for the individual we have been asked to pray for.

We can only speak words of Truth. For instance,...

What we know about the Sun is its expected rise each day. We also know that Sun shines all the time whether we see it or not. We know that the Life that orchestrates the Sun, governs our souls as well. For our souls are bonded to that Life more than the painter's paintings. We also know the Original sustains Itself and are not we incorporated with It? We remember the Breath of God is breathed at every point of Itself, in you and me and most assuredly in the form known as our dear friend Matt. We see them as they are, ever whole in their heart, mind and body. Yielding to and being completely uplifted by that Life that breathes all. We know this, feel this, reveal only this and rest in God. So it is. Amen.

THOUGHT #49

My Unfolding

I awake in gratitude. Immersed in much cognitive gyration. Attempting to coordinate, calibrate and consciously arrange the varied sounds and aromas of this day. As spring unfolds I find many sounds and shapes to intrigue me. Plenty of uniqueness.

Each one of us is different yet when and if we peer closer we will find brilliance beyond our perception and kinship of plentitude.

THOUGHT #50

Get Thee Out of Thy Country

Rabbi Zusya taught: God said to Abraham: "Get thee out of thy country, and from thy kindred, and from thy father's house, unto the land that I will show thee." God says to man: "First, get you out of your country, that means the dimness you have inflicted on yourself. Then out of your birthplace, that means, out of the dimness your mother inflicted on you. After that, out of the house of your father, that means, out of the dimness your father inflicted on you. Only then will you be able to go to the land that I will show you."

We find there are at least three steps leading to soulful liberty and Willingness is key.

THOUGHT #51

No Contradictions

From the Rabbi of Mogielnica: "It is well known that the sayings of our sages which seem to contradict one another are all 'words of the living God.' Each of them decided according to the depth of his root in Heaven, and up there all their words are truth, for in the upper worlds there are no contradictions. There, all opposites, such as prohibition and permission, guilt and guiltlessness, are one unified whole. The distinction between prohibition and permission appears only in their actions on earth.

We seek to live beyond polarity. Never again wanting the fruit of knowledge of good and evil.

THOUGHT #52

The Hidden Meaning in the Siren's Song

As the coyote howls in the night plotting the hills for those moonlight travelers, so our spirits are guided by the inaudible call of a Siren that our souls take note of. It is uncanny if we step back to see that spiritually the Siren's call, alluring as it may be, is not to attract us to a rocky shore but rather to alert us in Spirit's own gentle way of what to avoid. Remember Love speaks softly. For instance, we may hear the call as to avoid the rocky shore of emotional distress of a friend's obsessive-compulsive challenge. Infinite Wisdom actively gives Voice [for those who heed] as the Siren's call. For then suddenly life changes and what used to be perceived as an explosion in rage is seen simply as a cry for love. At these moments instead of rushing towards the call of rage ready to engage, we pause, drop anchor in the Deep and send lifeboats of love to that soul in need. We anchor our thoughts, words, and deeds deep into Spirit and remain quiet till we hear Stillness speak. All the while knowing the true perfection of that Being. Giving them all the room they need, as unconditionally loving as possible, to receive that lifeboat of love we send. If it is not accepted then we know we are not their channel for rescue and there is yet another for them. And since we have remained in that Deep abiding we easily shift our sails and proceed on course.

THOUGHT #53

There is Nothing Wrong with You!

"There is nothing wrong with you!" "Get off that floor!" "Stop your sniffling!"

"I will give you something to cry about!" "It is just a little scratch!"

The bottom line is there truly is nothing wrong with you.

People did things to us and we have done stuff to ourselves that has no lasting effect on who we ARE created in the image and likeness of. A Divine purpose of the prodigal son's freedom run was to liberate his thinking, which allowed him to experience his creatorship. Then realize that no matter how bad he messed up he could never undo WHO he was. He was his father's son – always. His father confirmed it and there were no lasting effects to his past actions. So instead of wishing for some future completion date when we might be more whole or perfect just realize there is nothing wrong with you. You are as complete as the Universe created you. We have not the power to Recreate ourselves in any other image. Only in the dim mirror of our miscreations (and words from a few well-meaning friends) do we see what would scare us. We see a blurred false expression of who we really are. And just to prove it go out and show YOUR DIVINITY... forgive yourself a long held hurt or regret, let someone know they are just like you who may have forgotten. Offer yourself in service. Find a way to bring up the joy level in life around you. You will begin to experience what Jesus also taught about these greater things you shall do. For there is nothing wrong with you!

THOUGHT #54

Ode to the Human Psyche

Today if you are touching any physical object, be it chair, computer or food send gratitude immediately to a trucker. They are on the roads under duress with tight delivery schedules and still they have to keep their wits about them. Frankly, aren't most of us keeping sanity just one scoop from a whole pot.

The resiliency of the human psyche is a study in amazement. Especially when we consider that some statistics reveal 1 in 4 Americans has had or will have a 'mental recess' of a significant nature during their lifetime. Yet our minds somehow keep it together.

We must admire the tenacity of a chronological 20-year-old a with a mental condition of age 6 whose big accomplishment for the day is getting fully dressed and tying their shoes successfully. Or how about the abandoned infant who becomes class valedictorian. What mental feats did either of these two make given their history especially if it was revealed to them.

There are bi-racial Vietnamese young adults still holding on despite being ostracized in their home society. Have we read the stories of human trafficking survivors and fumbled with our emotions hearing the details? Yet they can hold a conversation without weeping. Resilience? Yes!

It takes trading springtime stories with people living with cancer to appreciate operating in the realm called 'normal'. Needless to say, understanding the mental calculus of a man hoping to establish and maintain a heterosexual relationship after playing involuntarily the female role while in prison. Resilience? Sure!

The aforementioned situations may appear beyond what we call normal. However, it is somewhat 'normal' days for those souls. And for many of them to live out and beyond those circumstances is a tribute to what makes the human psyche so amazing. Yet there is another aspect that makes life better for our friends above and even us each day. Those are the works of holistic therapists, practitioners and light workers whose open hearts enable the healing to really begin!

THOUGHT #55

Mothertime

If there was a rock for each wonderful mother I personally know I could probably recast the tower of 'babble'. Meaning I have such vibrant inspiring memories of each one, that as I recollect I become as a young child with unformed words. Some mothers travel miles and oceans to visit their daughters. Some make sure their children get whatever it takes to graduate. Some encourage their children to move to new cities and take on challenges. Some make sure they have a super meal at least once a week. They send birthday cards and make lots of prayers too. My solemn feelings to every woman that wanted children and has not been able to conceive. Yet there is a principle of motherhood we all participate in moment by moment. We have an idea, a thought, a feeling, a worry, a resentment, a fear, a desire we nurse and nurture till it comes to fruition or drives us bonkers. Thank God for the principle of grace and unconditional love that never ceases to give us a fresh start. Thank God for mothers. Blessings to all in this season of remembrance.

THOUGHT #56

Our Real Nature

Today as you gaze at the translucent skies, the bright spring air enters your body. You breathe in even deeper. You let no drop of heaven's diamond mist escape. Whether you are at work or play or somewhere in between, glance around and see what atmosphere you are participating in. You are the one important part of the picture. You are the unique blending of the High Invisible with Its own soft, denser essence. You carry eternity within you. Because you exist, the History and the Memory of the Life that Is and Always Is stands in testimony of Its own progression.

The idea of evolutionary progress is a Divine one. As you breathe, the universe breathes also. Cells divide, stars collide and the earth spins. The progression of humanity is something more than we are collectively. The blending of breaths, beliefs, flesh, fabric, customs and cultures has assured us of an ever-evolving splendor of tapestry reflecting Spirit's fourth dimensionality. As above so below.

While you may carry forth characteristics from times gone before, your real nature is animated by Something mystics dream of, sages soulfully contemplate, and preachers peek at. It is called the Life of God in you, thru you and as you.

With the very next encounter you have with another soul in this third dimension, let them know, by glance or words, they are a unique way Life is expressing Itself and you see only the best in them and for them. Share your own eternal journey with them. The rainbow brings an array of color and a Promise!

THOUGHT #57

Meditation

Try, there is no try...   There is only do. – Asian Proverb

Trying to describe magic is like trying to cut a steak with a screwdriver. –Tom Robbins

There is no thought for today, only emptiness and allowing. – Lynn C.

So as thoughts come we will let them freely go. We will feel no attachment to them. We will enter into a quiet period during the rush of the day. Our hearts are set to enjoy the magic of the mystery of co-joining with the Omniverse. This is the period of time when we consciously seek to open a dialogue with Infinity. We want to be like a fish in the ocean, not trying to own it, just happy to be in it.

Meditation is the subject. The absence of active participatory thought, mind disengaged and cuddled to sleep. This is a time for our heart to share its accumulated cares and give them to the Father of lights, where they will be absorbed into the Great Beneficence out of our reach and concern.

This spiritual tool is followed in practically all spiritual paths and used seriously by the avatars and novices alike as the primary means of communing with the All That Is. Richard Shining Thunder Francis, a contemporary mystic describes meditation as 'not something we do, but something we stop doing.' Ultimately it becomes a moment when our persona ceases to exist. All that is left is our yielding inward soul posture delighting to hear the Voice of God.

Nothing scary about it, except to the ego, who thinks there is something to protect us from. As we begin, we learn to switch to being an observer of our thoughts. Watching them go by, without interfering. Most of us have experienced the mindless chatter which rattles our quiet time occasionally. Take heart if you can hear this chatter then know that the majority of your mind is actually silent. Else you wouldn't hear the chatter.

Finally, meditation is the harmless way to connect with our Divine Source. For in it, no matter how brief or extended, one experiences real communion within the holiest of sanctuaries – our hearts!

THOUGHT #58

Opening for Source

Everything about me proclaims the good of God almighty!

Peace by Peace the beloved community is anchored through me!

I live in alignment with God's big idea for my life!

My miracle consciousness blesses everyone I meet!

Divine and compelling right action orders my days and my ways!

Gracefully and gratefully I let it be!

And so it is! Amen!

Michael Bernard Beckwith – Founder and Spiritual Director, Agape International Spiritual Center

Question: Do I know how to be the opening for God Itself?

THOUGHT #59

To Make Our Mark

Often, I share with people whenever they see 'B+…' somewhere they know I have been there. Though I have yet to carve my initials into a tree or etch them in stone like Moses' God. Don't we all wish we could, unspoken desire or not, carve our names or other words into a living thing or even see our names in lights. How many of us have written the names of our first 'crush' on our school tablets or even on our jeans or better yet scratched their initials into our desks. We seem to have an innate desire to carve into that which we want to create, kind of like Source did in the beginning '…Let there be…' These may sound elementary nevertheless, they satisfy a desire to create and be known.

Whatever is carved into a tree grows and goes as long as the tree lives. Or is it better to put one's initials or declarations of love on moving objects that travel from coast to coast? Some railroad car artwork is very well done – if I had to have an opinion. I noticed the other day; these creative geniuses rarely paint over the important markings used by the rail industry. Maybe this is evidence that creativity can co-exist within the context of the organized intellect. Let's not talk about the etchings we see at roadside rests!

There are numerous ways that we create or intentionally promote the desires of our hearts. Some are cries for help and others are simply 'Kilroy was here'. Our 'image and likeness' nature affords us a grand opportunity to carve into the invisible. We trust in the Source that is growing the Tree that our initials and declarations of love continue to move and expand. Just think if we could carve our initials into a beanstalk and then climb to visit the Giant who loves us very much. Wouldn't that be the best of both worlds?

Please remember to create responsibly!

THOUGHT #60

A Declaration of Compassion

Do you ever feel a desire to be there for everyone? The recent weeks in my life have felt that way. Of late my life has been filled with concerns – not overboard – just caring for and being available for others.

I have exhausted sleep time in meditation, phone discussions, text, and personal conversations all to the upliftment of friends and souls whom I am barely consciously familiar with. All to which I am humbled and grateful for!

And I have given each one of them tears of joy for their breakthroughs, tears for their pain, be it self-inflicted or not, and tears of sadness when I feel helpless to do more.

Recently I sat with a dear friend who is having an incredible walk in this life. As we discussed some important personal discoveries in their life I let myself become disinterested. They noticed and fortunately we were able to resume sincere conversation.

After that I went to my upper room and wept. Thank God and the grand design of the body to shed emotions through tears. I shed tears for them, and also for myself for a couple of reasons. For a moment I had put myself into a cage with the rope out of reach. This rope represented connection to a world outside my secured inner self – to the world of interpersonal loving support. They needed it and I could not give it. That moment of impasse shocked me to an awareness of how many souls inside our lives and across the planets need that connection. Need someone to be open for them.

Perhaps it starts with freeing the crow trapped by a plastic bag in the morning, to prosperity visioning with the family man recently laid off, to giving healing energy for a co-worker who wants to be pain free, to sharing with people who want better nutrition for their families, to dialoguing with children learning to play well with others, to working with grownups struggling to find and answer their call in life, to cultivating my own personal evolution in the consciousness of love.

As a wonderful therapist friend of mine asks often 'who is there for you?' Today I add to it 'and who are you there for?'

Let your life be the Unceasing Prayer.

THOUGHT #61

Seek the Higher Thought

"You can't solve a problem with the same thinking that caused it." Albert Einstein

Today we embrace that feeling of an opening into which we commit our hearts, minds and souls. The body will come along. A little fear yes, but nowhere near a level to impede our progress into a grander version of ourselves. We follow a vision given only to us and as needed to those who become part of that plan for a better life. As above so below!

The High Thought is one of harmony and understands our innate beginning, our Infinite Heritage. Of choosing not to have an opinion to the best of our ability assures us of staying in alignment with that High Thought. She leads us safely away from the infamous tree of good and evil and into a new way of thinking so that we might really experience the Tree of Life.

Today we step out of mediocrity and into a strange sunlight. A Single Light that shines on us from above casting a full color spectrum of our incarnate self onto the water and long into the sand beneath the water at the shoreline. It appears as if we are deeply tied into this earthly dimension, being swiftly changed by the recession of the next wave. However, a second solid shadow is cast before us. The High Thought walks before us, showing our soul's evolutionary pattern. The body follows. We see that with each step we are willing to give ourselves, our past dissolves in the Light. Our present self is in constant transitory movement and our future becomes clearly defined.

Today let's breathe slowly and deeply as we allow ourselves to think a High Thought. She is there holding the strange light in the opening that we must take to experience what Life is waiting to share with us. Selah.

THOUGHT #62

A Rabbit's Nature

A Rabbit's nature is so multi-prolific that it is always available to Itself! It replicates itself more frequently and numerically than anything that would seek to consume it. Sure, consumers moving into an area may seem to reduce the numbers, yet there is always a remnant.

We daily have interactions with people who are beset with a portion of negative energy. How do we handle such encounters: avoid them, join them, or offer some tender, high vibration food to them? Help them multiply the high thoughts.

Those who study food from a nutritional perspective know that raw, dark green leafy vegetables are high in anti-oxidants for aging and immunity values to thwart disease. These foods are very high vibration. As rabbits eat this high vibration food, they can't help but share it with others. By offering themselves they distribute life-sustaining power. Those consumers who feed on them are unconsciously 'getting the good stuff' - the high vibration food. I am not advocating eating meat rather illustrating the interconnectivity of all life.

Now I offer this parallel for consideration. Let's say rabbits are everywhere and seem to be an excellent high vibration food source. A metaphysical view is that God is everywhere, sustains all and is our health to the degree we recognize our Oneness. We can never run out of God or rabbits. Is God the rabbit always available to Itself? Is It the high vibration food that is portion dependent [the more you consume of God the better off you are]? Is It the consumer who values the high vibration of the rabbit? Is It the Ever-Giving Nature expressed by the rabbit?

You see as we contemplate these questions and answer them truthfully, we will find the old confines of what God is and where God can be found gets a little blurry. We will find there simply is nowhere God is not. Thank God!

Summarily, if All That Is comes from a Single Source and there is no other creator then All That Is comes from that Allness and conclusively must be prolific in its multiplicity of form and function by Its own implicit and explicit nature. God could then be alternatively defined as the rabbit influencing Life by Giving its high vibration Self away and never running short on Itself.

THOUGHT #63

Turtle Love

What causes the turtle to withdraw into its shell? Is it the denial of the anticipated future or fear in its mind? Or are there perceived dangers? Real or imagined the turtle reacts to the threat by pulling in all exposed parts. Thus, presenting us a practical example in the practice of noninterference. Whatever 'little green monster' has appeared in its conscious awareness gets very little interaction or confrontation from our shelled friend. By observation it appears that friend or foe is treated the same. By first going within the turtle allows time for perceived foes to exhaust and grow weary of their initial interest, re-emerging with a renewed sense of wellbeing from its High Plateau. By going within first before reappearing towards a friend, it brings out fresh agape love.

Our days in life bring us in contact with all sorts of active energies and objectives some which we may not want to entertain. A lesson in turtle love may be helpful to enter into. Noninterference offers us a way to move ahead without involving ourselves in others agendas unnecessarily. Turtle love will not dissuade another from their journey nor give them reason to doubt their direction as understood by themselves (noninterference).

When situations come near that cause us some measure of alarm, swiftly recall turtle love, turn inward and re-emerge with that sacred glow from having communed with your own higher Self then proceed – freely and fearlessly forward!

Happy wandering!

THOUGHT #64

Let Love

Love is a quintessential reality. It lives in the face of awesome brutality and even squalor. It is latently alive behind the faces of sad happy people. We know them, happy faces, yet as we study them a certain sad vibration begins to echo its painful tone even in us.

Nothing builds Love, it happens. It takes letting and allowing. It is true that one must decide to allow love. In that process of allowing sometimes even momentarily a twinkle of it is born into whatever situation a person may be facing. The experience of it grows in proportion to the constant attention to how it operates without us doing anything.

Subjective love can trigger many highs and many low qualities. Objectively Love can be pursued as if by hounds from hell and never be arrived at because its place is deep within our hearts. When our hearts open, it comes forth sharing Its glory.

It may not immediately alter circumstances but It will put us in a safe place. A place of nonjudgment, emotional and mental limberness and release. Both a release from our hold to a perception of reality or trying to force an outcome or manipulate a situation. Love asks us to let it be. Let it be the activity of our consciousness that sets us free.

THOUGHT #65

I am Healed

There is a story of two lovers. One felt strongly that they could not trust the other even though there was no major episode to justify this. The woman wanted the man to trust her judgment in seemingly a lot of things. Conversely, he desired the same of her. How would you compromise on that?

A Course in Miracles Lesson #137 teaches 'when I am healed I am not healed alone'. The learner learns as their perceptions are liberated they will not hold another in bondage. Another coveted scripture admonishes 'you will be judged with the same measure from which you judge'. Meaning the standard we judge another is the same standard we will come under and does not have to be the same circumstances but you will get that same feeling.

It stands to reason of universal application that to receive what we desire from others is to offer the same. One cannot exhale without an inhale. Gandhi asks us to be the change we wish to see. I believe the principle that stands so clear is to set the personal standard to do to others what you would have them do to you. We should not give what we would choose not to receive. We are talking of transcendent transactions not trinkets or birthday gifts; those standards that make for living a high frequency sanctified life. If that is trust, then find it first within yourself and give it. Don't let the world make you a hologram of its egoic perceptions. You will not die when you choose the Life giver and listen to the Voice for God. It is intrinsic in the fabric from which you are woven to be able to do this. Hold your perceptions up to the light of Truth and you will be humbled yet safe.

THOUGHT #66

Love's Presence

There I was in her presence again. Each day is fresh and new with her. Her manner is always welcoming and lifts one above the anticipated grind of the day. I always feel stronger when we make eye contact. I am always so glad to know she is here. Not just for what she does for my life but for everyone whom she comes in contact with. What would the world do without such souls as hers? It seems as if loving is her vocation.

Relationships have no boundaries. We are all part of someone's or something's existence. We interact with animate and inanimate objects constantly. The tangible and intangible. From rocks to chairs to thoughts to people, we have formed relationships. If we are asked what type of relationship we have with each and every, or they were asked …what would the response be?

The question is …is our lovingness as attractive and healthily radiant as my friend who works as clerk in a convenient store. We want to get to a place where people simply love our presence because It is Love's Presence.

THOUGHT #67

Where the Heart Is

As we look around we see Life has been better than not to us. Excepting sudden weather changes no walls are collapsing on us for unexplained reasons, trees are not chasing us down the street nor are Lilliputians shooting fiery darts at us. So why are we so unsettled emotionally in our hearts. We know not all our circumstances or situations are the same. Some people have their dining rooms underneath freeway overpasses while others have 'model' homes in so-called exclusive secure neighborhoods.

Regardless of location, the constant seems to be the same – a place that offers personal space for self and even a family. The cardboard box or the brick structure offer something called 'home'. Home has been described as 'where the heart is'. If this is true what are we as a society saying when we build more heart specialty centers? To what do we owe the increase to? Is this indicative of a fact that we do not know where our 'heart' is and thus are not at home with ourselves? ...within ourselves?

THOUGHT #68

Who's Talking

When we feel we have given our all, we should ask 'who's talking?' We know this may sound difficult when it is our intellect talking and feels it knows everything. Ironically the difficulty lies in accepting the limits our little minds have imposed.

Oftentimes this means breaking ranks with ourselves. The intellect will assume it has covered all the bases, checked every angle, and forded every stream. It may tell us we have exhausted all means and there is nothing more we can do to solve a problem, to improve our certainty for an impassioned course of action or even save ourselves from some anticipated dilemma.

Here enters the Deep Inner Self who speaks to us at the point of our exasperation. It does not chide us for self-condemnatory platitudes. It greets us, explaining that we are exactly where we need to be – exhausted of intellectualized ideas, momentum, mental and physical resources. The Deep Inner Self knows what will have to be shown to the intellect, so singular Peace once held in heart and mind returns.

THOUGHT #69

Kicking the Illusion

The next time you watch a soccer match contemplate this. The soccer ball is an illusion. It is like so many things in life we pick up and play with such as feelings of not enough, feelings of being broke (all forms), habits, dis-eases, religious judgement, etc. Just kicking it around has no effect towards any good thing. It might occupy us for a while, we may even find it fun. Yet putting it in the end zone is the object that makes the whole GAME. In other words, we can sweat the illusion or we can kick the livin' out of it and make it work for us.

Signed Rich and Happy (two long lost brothers)

THOUGHT #70

Compliments to the Chef!

From the time we came into this dimensionality we learned to create a reaction in others whether we did it by screaming or crying. We experienced the reflection of approval or look of fear or disbelief. And then we grew up... well maybe.

Except now it is our turn to experience the reaction from others in a grown-up way of shock and awe of disbelief and denial. And the trigger to get it all started is as simple as a sincere compliment. Spontaneous words of appreciation and acknowledgement seem to catch some folks off guard. So much that they will deny what we say is true, discounting our intelligence and openness or better yet make a joke of it. 'Better put your boots on' is often the comment. They are saying that because what we are saying is getting deep like poop.

I would suggest adding one or two more affirmative appreciation phrases after the initial hoopla stops. It seems to let others know we are 'crazy' about how this person does their work and exists as a unique individuation of Creativity.

What you may notice after this point is how that person begins to work and respond to you. There becomes a heightened sense of attention to their tasks as they internally start grading their own paper with all sorts of great questions like: 'am I really that good', 'do I really mean that much', 'how else can I get these positive strokes', what else can I do'... etc, etc.

What has happened is a deepening of the bond between two souls. In a very clever and concealed way we are saying 'Namaste'.

THOUGHT #71

Waking Up

When we awake it is a time of reunion. The soul returns to behold its beloved and rouses it to more conscious living and interaction.

Being conscious of the state of awakening we feel and test our body's capability to move. It is always good to ensure that the soul is completely back in the body before trying to move.

It is the parallel to the physical waking process that we really want to look at. Are the natural tendencies when we wake up the same for our unfoldment in the other areas of our lives? Do we have a need to first eliminate? Eliminate wasteful ideas, concepts or 'stuff'. Do we feel a need to breathe in fresh air into our emotions? Or do we look outside to see how to prepare for the weather. Or do we get out of bed, stretch and get into a yoga position. Some of us probably do all of these.

Just whatever we do when we 'wake up' can be indicative of how we undertake our spiritual unfoldment or any other areas of life. Now only we can know our wake-up patterns and determine how they may or may not be the most beneficial patterns for us. How many times are we pushing snooze on our consciousness awakening?

THOUGHT #72

Experience, Understanding and Wisdom

Many say nothing beats a cool glass of water on a hot day. Ducks may say nothing beats a rainy day.

For all of us existing in Consciousness we share multitudes of perspectives whose variance is reflective of the many navigational points plotted by the Hubble and other space scopes.

They observe, unfiltered all they receive, similar to our eyes or the lens of a camera. These mechanisms are not the judgment or opinion–makers for they are neutral. We use this information to build our lives.

In the case of Eve from the Bible's Genesis story, she uses at least 3 of the senses: sight, touch and taste. She suffered because she formed an opinion lacking Knowledge and Understanding from experience. Therefore, formed a perspective that gave no basis for wisdom. Or was her learning experience abruptly terminated? Clearly, she may have made different choices if she was allowed to have a do-over.

We love Eve because she demonstrates so clearly that understanding comes from experience and knowledge from understanding.

For the sake of embracing Knowingness, we forsake our perspectives. We become open to more than facts or figures. We forsake all others and cling to Truth.

THOUGHT #73

The Art of Getting

'It's far easier for any person to say, "I'm going to make a million dollars" and succeed, than to say "I'm going to attain spiritual light "and succeed. It is far easier to accomplish anything in the human world than in the spiritual, because in the spiritual life we are called upon to die before we can gain what we're seeking. Don't ever forget that: you have to die before you can gain your spiritual life. You don't gain it by giving up smoking or drinking or eating meat. You don't gain it by studying for a few years or having some classes. Whew! If only it were that easy! You give it up by dying daily. Every single day of the week some trace of humanhood leaves us and is sent about its business in the world of appearances. Every problem is an opportunity to spiritually resolve whatever the situation may be.'

Joel S. Goldsmith *The Foundation of Mysticism* p. 317

Our getting is found in the letting. We obtain what we make room for in our heart-minds.

THOUGHT #74

Truth About Truth

Dark clouds and mists do not deter the seeker of truth for at least two reasons.

The seeker searches for firmness underlying the mists where their eyes may not venture. Secondly the truth is a lover that wants to be found. She is found in the simple mechanics of an anthill as well as in the dark cloud's existence. Truth is what lies beyond perception.

THOUGHT #75

On Rightness

In answer to the question, "What kind of life do you envision for yourself?" Tara Singh responded:

"Rightness

Rightness is independent of personality and its consequences.

It stands vertical – a law unto itself.

Nothing of the body senses can affect or obscure it. Rightness is independent of the limitations of right and wrong, thus free of judgment and conflict, free of lack, of seeking and trying, free of thought, feelings, and reactions. Such a man is liberated from the illusion of time and its beliefs and concepts. Ever stable, stately and uninvolved, he knows no loss, gain, or unfulfillment. Such a man is an extension of the grace of God. He has an atmosphere of purity surrounding him. It is a blessing to be in his presence and have the ears to hear his eternal Words." Tara Singh: *Nothing Real Can Be Threatened* p. 261-2

We are that! We are what lies beyond judgment. Whole and complete.

THOUGHT #76

Knowing Life Rightly

As I sit and wait for insights from Spirit, I reflect upon the gods', little god's and the Supreme's blessings to me. This period of reflection finds me unreserved and willing to look at all the peaches Unadulterated Life has given. Resultantly all I have learned leads me to a simple conclusion that God provides the meat of the peach for my present life as well as the pit for future growth. Thus, we give thanks for our daily bread with the knowing that buried deep in each blessing (should we choose to see them) is a seed, a symbol of still more goodness to come. So, the guiding question is not so much are we living each day as if it were our last rather are we treating each day as if we want to see the next?

THOUGHT #77

Gambling

The 13th century poet Rumi stated "Gamble everything for Love"

"Gamble everything for Love, if you're a true human being. If not, leave this gathering.

Half-heartedness doesn't reach into majesty. You set out to find God, but then you keep stopping for long periods at mean–spirited roadhouses."

Love wins because **It** is an Eternal Power not a temporal force.

THOUGHT #78

Be You

If you are ever asked to look across your work organization for a mentor what would you say or who would you select? Let's widen the scope – say across the whole company or wider still people in like vocations in organizations around the world. Maybe we have a mentor already in our vocation. If we don't, odds are we could find one in the world of our more soulful practices. Then when we find one, how closely are we going to model ourselves after that person?

The degree to which we model ourselves after someone else may actually be of lesser value than if we seek to be fuller expressions of our own rich, unique selves. Even when we learn from others we end up adding our own style.

Real progress is made by how we apply what was learned in an adaptive process. What Martin Luther King Jr. learned from Gandhi was applied in the United States with different dynamics with yet similar results – a significant shift in the social landscape. Summarily as we look across the horizon of learnedness, we see landmark principles that can be applied and experienced in varied settings with comparable results. We call these 'truth' principles or eternal verities. Someone has to model them. Like water, we find it everywhere and it is composed of the same elements having the same capabilities. Dr. David Hawkins (Truth vs. Falsehood) states "Truth stands on its own". It does not need corroboration or help to be. Truth just is.

So today be you, love yourself and be in truth a unique expression of all the Wonder there is. Be the twinkle in God's eye.

THOUGHT #79

To Love Without

A Sufi mystic sees an empty food sack hanging on a nail and becomes excited to an ecstatic level. Soon joined by others, the whole gathering grows into a stirring holy moment. They chant "Food for what needs no food! A cure for hunger."

A passerby, having no insight to the cause for celebration, said to them "It's an empty sack!" The Sufi decried the comment, telling the person to leave, they were not a lover.

The Sufi says "A lover's food is the love of bread, not the bread. No one who really loves, loves existence.

Lovers have nothing to do with existence. They collect the interest without the capital." – Rumi

To love without having the object may be somewhat unique to us. This may even seem quite ludicrous. Yet Rumi assures us we are quite sane to allow ourselves to rise above attachments. The Sufi mystic suggests that we move away from that place where the object controls our love and ability to be free. We arrive at a new place where love is given from within most joyously and just having something that we want can be the real goal. Our loving becomes the measuring stick and not that which is to be measured. We love for love's sake and for no other reason. Thus, what we have been given freely can be freely given.

THOUGHT #80

Loving Objectively

Many of us have sat on up half the night with a friend, working to overcome some obstacle of importance to them. We also know of or have experienced the world of tutoring children. Then after countless hours of worry and attention they make the passing mark. Maybe we have helped a friend financially over and over again till we can't and then they die leaving nothing to return to us but the ideas of generosity and beneficence. These circumstances beg the question of how much kindness we can offer. Perhaps a clue is if we start to feel like we are in a tug-of-war with our friend.

Somewhere during the dynamic course of events our role shifts. We find ourselves no longer helping them pull the baby from the lion's jaws but contending with them to which side of the lion's mouth the baby will be pulled from. Meanwhile neither the lion nor whatever the circumstance is, is made less severe by our positioning.

Relax and don't take it personal just remember to ask yourself, who's issue it? Are we operating from a place of nonattachment? Meaning while we hope the best, we are not vested in a particular outcome except for our friend's highest good. Their good may not be what we perceive it to be. We are there for them, holding Love's watch. We are mindful that we can't help a turtle if they keep withdrawing or insist on keeping the issue with them.

THOUGHT #81

Sheba's Throne

'When the Queen of Sheba came to Solomon she left behind her kingdom and her wealth the way lovers leave behind their reputations......

... Solomon saw that her heart was open to him and that her throne she insisted on bringing would soon become repulsive to her "Let her bring it", he said...

When you see the splendor of union, the attraction of duality seems poignant and lovely, but much less interesting.' –Rumi

One thing this story symbolizes is Beauty and Riches of this world falling in love with Wisdom and attempting to bring a remnant of its present life into its New Life. Wisdom obliges because it knows that eventually Beauty will find its old throne no longer suitable as it grows in enlightenment. What once gave us a sense of power and comfort has little or no value in the New Life.

THOUGHT #82

Ruby

The Sunrise Ruby – Rumi

The transparency of the ruby allows the sunlight to shine through it. This spiritual practice must become a daily discipline if we are to let more of THAT WHICH IS shine through us.

In the early morning hour, just before
dawn, lover and beloved wake and
take a drink of water.

She asks, "Do you love me or yourself
more?

Really, tell me the absolute truth."

He says, "There is nothing left of me.

I'm like a ruby held up to the sunrise.
Is it still a stone, or a world

made up of redness? It has no
resistance to sunlight."

....The ruby and the sunrise are
one. Be courageous and discipline
yourself...

work, keep digging your well.

Don't think about getting off from
work.

Water is there somewhere.

Submit to a daily practice. Your loyalty to that is a ring on the door.

Keep knocking and the joy inside will eventually open a window and
look out to see who's there.

THOUGHT #83

Patience

Patience. What a word. A very popular one too! Used often and
preached about endlessly.

How much do we understand what we are asking others to do when
say 'have patience, it is a virtue you know.'

From a young age we are given a variety of situations from which we
are to learn about patience. But how does one actually define a virtue?

What are patience's parameters and structural components? We can learn the concept of sitting in traffic or pacing the floor or sitting and waiting, etc, etc. But the truth of the matter is there are no set rules to teach patience.

How long is patience? Do we set a standard of one hour in traffic? 3 hours for baby delivery. Do we create a 7-minute rule of patience for children watching fresh baked cookies coming out of the oven? How long is enough?

Let's face it, your mom's idea of patience and your cousin's were not the same. Patience and several other terms like 'pride' we use often cannot be taught; only experienced in context. Perhaps we can teach people how to learn it for themselves using certain situations as examples. By doing so we can liberate ourselves and society from the tyranny of the subjective patience rule. We free others to create their own measurable standard for how long they will abide in a given situation so guilt or blame do not become part of that formula when they decide they have had enough *patience*!

THOUGHT #84

The Idea Of Mateship

THE IDEA OF MATESHIP is actually that one thought cannot be complete by itself. It is complete in itself, yet to exist consciously another thought must receive it and complete it. This completing thought makes creation possible.

The individual thought contains within itself an activity, something contemplated, a cosmic record. The singular thought is now in relationship, having begun movement from the subjective to the objective. In order for the mateship to progress smoothly, the beginning thought must realize it is not being sacrificed, and is truly beneficial for its purpose. It is being transmuted and amplified.

In short one thought leads to another like unto itself. The mateship occurs as the completing thought conceives of the leading thought. The result is signified in the field of objectivity, form or experience. Presenting us with a new look of an old phrase: A man (subjective thought) shall cling unto his wife (conception principle/thought) and the two shall become one (objective law activated).

THOUGHT #85

Emotional Availability

The livingness and givingness of nature seems to flow effortlessly this time of year thanks to the birds. The early morning symphony heralds the Presence, dawning of each new day. They speak of flowers beds to shop, new partners to meet and other such matters of avian interest. Their openness to share uncompromisingly reminds me to be emotionally present. Reckon this may be a little stunning if you like peeking through the blinds directly into the fresh sunlight.

Nonetheless I have found emotional availability (EA) key to building better relationships with strong underpinnings. People experience our givingness through feelings that we are there for them. They feel it consciously and unconsciously.

Our EA is reflected in posture, sound, actions and words (may or may not be used). Of real importance is treating the person and that moment like it matters. There is plenty more that could be said about EA but frankly the sounds of birds say a beak's full. So, if you are wanting a relationship or one that floats smoother, practice saying to others 'care to share' and watch for a different reaction as now it is you leaning forward being receptive.

THOUGHT #86

Awareness from the Unconscious

Ever heard the phrase: Whose life is it anyway?

Actually, this rings true for most of us. Our actions, mannerisms, likes and dislikes are for the most part learned. Consciously and unconsciously picked up thru earlier life. When we want to change, or see something we want, perhaps if we asked 'why' the reason may be surprising. For instance, let's say one or both of our parents were very overbearing. We look along the chain of our relationships and what do we see, dominant people. Realize this discussion is general and may not apply to you, just your friends!

Spoke with a friend recently that wanted his home to have a door facing each direction. After years of trying to convince his wife and friends that should be done he stumbled upon the reason why. When he was describing his boyhood home to a friend magically the 'why' came to his awareness.

The home he grew up in was functionally designed that way. The unconscious had been driving his preference for years and he had no idea where it came from. So what other areas of life might be under unconscious influence for you or your friends.

Of course, now he knows where the desire came from he can examine it with fresh eyes and new understanding. If this ever happens to your friends here are some helps: How is this desire serving you at this point of awakening? Does it still make sense? Is it time for new information?

Remember some of us wakeup quickly and others like to sleep-in. So just have gratitude when you discover the 'bear' of your unconscious coming out of the woods in your conversations ['bear' as described in Ted Andrews' book *Animal Speak*].

THOUGHT #87

Faith Walk

Most creative minds and those of us who lend ourselves to creative influxes, find that the 99 percent solution is outside our immediate frame of reference or awareness. We realize there is some issue, some dilemma, some wrinkle in life that needs a 'fix'. We may feel there is a way but don't know how. Rest assured all is ok. We do not need to know the 'hows'. That is not our job nor are we that smart. Let us remember today to let Infinite Wisdom, Intuition, Holy Spirit, angels, etc do the work of figuring it all out and just be ready and open to follow.

Yes, walking by faith is a walk on the wild side because sometimes the solution is down a road less travelled.

See you on the other side of the mountain!

THOUGHT #88

The Body Kingdom

One aspect of Kabbalistic teachings describes the unblemished nature of humanity as 'sparks' of the All That Is. Today you are encouraged to view your body as a collection of those sparks as well. For in each cell there is a Divine program that defies complete explanation or replication. The cell is complete in itself but not by itself. Each one carrying forth as contained within, a full portion of the whole. So, praise the cells that make up the eyelids to the nail beds. Knowing that each is Holy because it is Holy wholly made. There is no other Source for Life. The 'sparks' are present – they sense –they build – they replace themselves under activity governed by an Eternal perpetual Law. Orchestrated as the heavens, declaring and decreeing how great thou art that the Creator is mindful of thee. Let that feeling run through your body kingdom awhile each hour, each second if you like. Speak love to the body – let it blow gently on the sparks of Divinity contained within to build that Holy Fire.

THOUGHT #89

Living from the Inside Out

It only stands to reason that the eyes and the liver are linked. What is not filtered by sight, insight or perception in the personal mind, will most assuredly have to be filtered by the liver. Let go toxic living and conditions.

We live from the inside out. Jesus taught it is not so much what a person eats that defiles them rather what comes from the inward parts. So, have a happy liver and thought cleansing day!

THOUGHT #90

Weak Timber

Nothing reveals the full load of the weight of any physical object like the weakest timber in a bridge span. When our oxcart of life is full to the brim with our wantings, our fat emotions and heavy hearts we must accept that everything we normally rely upon can take the weight. The situation points to the weakest timbers but they are not the enemy, they are the road sign. The situation is telling us we have too much baggage or should take a different path. The bridge has supported others yet at this particular time our load presents a challenge to our further progress in life.

Most of the time we have not felt the need to rush ahead of ourselves to check for weak timbers and replace them. We only discover them when our unique load is applied at that location, at that time.

At this point we should not become upset or disappointed, rather feel gratitude to the Universe for awareness of this pause point. We appreciate however long OR not this chance to see the effect of all our baggage. We realize that even though that particular weakness may be a person close to us they are responsible unto themselves. They are part of the many bridges we cross in life and fortunately we do not own the bridges only our baggage.

THOUGHT #91

Knowledge of Good and Evil

There were many trees in the garden. Much like there are opinions, beliefs and doctrines. Yet one thing remains the same, man will seek to do harm over what he believes is right. When we think we have the knowledge of good from evil we are attempting to draw a fuzzy line at best where darkness stops and light begins. We cannot seem to let go of that forbidden tree. How big is your opinion of a thing?

THOUGHT #92

To Ascend

When we find ourselves with head slightly tilted in upward glance, we know in a quick geographic second, we must be at the lower part of the landscape

Consequently, the horizon seems above us. It calls to us as where we would prefer to be. We see a level to ascend to.

The muddling parts of our life may temporarily knock us down and even capture our attention. Yet we know in a nanosecond this is not where we want to be. To ascend is the inner call.

In short, if we are looking at the mountains then it means we are probably in the valley. Unless we are finding gold there or something of benefit then better we head for the hills. To ascend is the better objective.

THOUGHT #93

The Idle Mind's Gift

It has been said 'an idle mind is the devil's workshop'. Of course, most of us on the Path know that the mind is hardly idle. We hear it having its own conversations while we are settling in for meditation or just out strolling. We also know that if there is a vacuum the Universe will fill it. This actually is a perfect scenario – spiritual enlightenment 101. Empty the mind and fill it with high virtues and eternally scented oils. We let it consume all fruits and garden yields of the holiest kinds.

Michael Roads, the humorous Australian writer of *True Prosperity* shares how the energetic vibration of whatever movie we watch carries on long past the credits. No need to guess where those vibrations find haven - within our psyche and our body. That if allowed become the dominant subtle news program our body feeds on.

One way of finding out what is playing in the mind's theater is to listen to it. Calmly allow it to stream during the quiet periods. Then gently begin to consciously insert thoughts of Truths; The

Lord is my shepherd… I shall not want…I come from Infinite Love and Intelligence… We want the quiet, 'idle' mind available to us as need be.

THOUGHT #94

We are Not Broken but Emerging

To the extent of the tears that may drip through our fingers to our toes; To the pangs of our loudest quiet screams of abandonment, and tastes of the forlorn, there is somehow a distilling of the disturbing distorted news or outlook.

Thereafter a period of momentary lapse of our faith power that normally rides astride a shining black charger, there comes a reckoning of sorts.

It is in this moment Truth and clarity we gain. For we realize it is only our outer shell that is cracked and we are but young ones emerging into a new paradigm nurtured by the light from the crack itself. Yet for an instant we thought we were broken.

THOUGHT #95

The Shoe

We learn early in this life about numbers and the placement of them. Regardless of the location or mathematical breakdown in an equation numbers are place holders in this dimension for quantifying and measuring. Depending on how we arrange them and what principles of truth are applied we can obtain significantly different outcomes. Often such is the case of our appeals to heaven commonly referred to as prayer.

Many of us were taught a manner of prayer by well-intentioned parents and teachers. How wonderful a job they performed! We should thank them earnestly. As the story goes they were also taught.

If we construct an equation where a Shoe represents the nature, habit or attitude of prayer handed down thru the centuries what would that outcome look like. Let the foot represent the understanding. The Shoe was shaped by some predecessors understanding of themselves and their relationship to the Allness centuries ago. Now if that understanding was born out of a life of slavery or harsh conditions would not those relevant factors reflect by associative property both of the nature of the prayee and of the Source prayed to. In this case God could be viewed as a taskmaster that would be moved by cries for mercy.

The image of God is carved in the sand of our misery or our inspired delight, and the outcome is assured no matter how awkwardly the prayer is put together. Today we rest in God knowing that your prayers are answered because for centuries we have been trying on the Shoe with our best understanding and reshaping it. Strangely enough the Almighty has heard it and responded. Never doubt how you fit with God just know that the Shoe fits! Pray without ceasing.

THOUGHT #96

Dating Silence

Many people spend all sorts of hours campaigning for a new look in their life. They are just not comfortable in their appearance, their home, their social status, their significant relationships, etc. We know them; they have to have the television going while they 'sleep', or music or news in the background constantly. It is as if their mind is on 'crank', a form of street drug that compels the body to keep going till exhaustion or terminal collapse. It is often we find them at wits end about way too many things of the daily life. Our friends have yet to make the connection between Silence and Sanity and Supremacy over one's life.

Ever take a walk early in the morning before even the first wave of workers head towards their daily tasks. Notice the sounds with no limitations. We can hear all sorts of things; most importantly we hear ourselves, our hearts, our breathing, our steps, our thoughts. Add in the hushing late night blanket of silence and perhaps some dense fog, to really experience a different orgasmic high. Men would do themselves a vital favor by allowing for such free adventures as joining with the Silence in Her many ways of being. They can reclaim their Sanity as God given and regain that mastery over their attitudes of present and previous needs and desires. Experience has taught me what a real game changing event this is to sit with Silence and feel Her as the Universe speaking. But She will not compete with technology for it is Her that gives such ideas to us. Every inventor knows this. For they have dated Her repeatedly and become saner and provided much to many. They show renewed virility of life and of service. They are better men for following Her Silence to a place of Sanity that leads to Supreme Realization. Take a walk on the real wild side where it is really quiet and you will feel the Peace of mind and health you have been searching for. I guarantee She is there!

THOUGHT #97

Eternal Link

What we give is never the totality of what we have for at least two reasons. One, we do not comprehend what we really have to offer in terms of our capacities or potentials. Secondly, probably the most exciting yet underviewed, is we are eternally linked to the Infinite and Its' Endless Potentiality. As Life goes about perfecting Itself in us, through us and as us, things and outcomes are changed. The shadows of a circumstance shift.

See you after the Theory of Relativity is over!

THOUGHT #98

The Gushing Faucet

Regardless of all the so-called facts we have in hand, all the beliefs we have, all the wrongs we hold against ourselves, all the questions we have, there is just no way to turn off the faucet. We have cringed, we have lied, we have imitated, we have feared and we are free. We have blown, popped and stuck bubble gum somewhere 'not proper' and we are still here. We have experienced cuts, bruises, births and deaths, rewards, awards, tricks from friends and hidden delights of all kinds. The beat goes on. We did not start it and we will not finish it. We have no say in that. Safely tucked away in our soul is the Self-eject button. But in order to get to it we must find the shutoff to the Ever-gushing Faucet. Lots of luck with that! Remember Life is a great tool for handling the day to day problems. The beat goes on...

THOUGHT #99

The Response

The Infinite awaits an eternal response from you today. It has waited and will always be available. It will be magnified through you, by your response. So, relax in the Everlasting arms and live abundantly.

THOUGHT #100

Snows of Life

Fresh look at the footprints in yesterday's snows

snows of who we've met, where we met,

things collected, things let go.

We look back

with advantage of being in the present.

Our steps reflect the journey, were they hurried,
were they heavy, were they light,

were they tiny, were they stretched long?

Our advantage now is present. We can continue. We
will continue when we decide we can decide.

We realize

yesterday's vision was our path to today.

Our advantage is now creativity.

Fear a useful yardstick.

How daring were our tracks of yesterday;

how bold the dreams for our next steps.

Fear lets us know

there is somewhere we want to go.

Be it signpost or roadblock

how shall we continue our tomorrows

in the fresh new snows of life...

– Coz Ruthles

THOUGHT #101

The Prankster's Demise

No amount of rascaldom will ever fill us up. The prankster will have the last prank but they by Law of Recompensation will be receivers of that which they garden. The jokester in his funny wrath, laughs himself right into the 'dip' (as seen in Roger Rabbit).

I knew of a prankster that worked in a microfilm department of a sizable bank. In the particular department he worked in, he was the best prankster. He could have pictures of a person coming out of the copier or walk around the office with 'kick me please I am the bad habit' posted on their back and other such daily unnerving things trying to get a laugh. Poor soul must have really been unsettled inside. After a while 'karma' went into effect. His co-workers were presented the right opportunity. Just as he was preparing to run an errand from their 6th floor office suite to the main lobby of the bank, he got a phone call so he rushed back to his desk to take the call. While he was on the phone one co-worker crafted a handy sign to be hung on his back. Another co-worker had the responsibility to hang it on the prankster as he rushed exiting the office. This was done under the guise of going to the restroom that were near the elevators in the hallway. The co-worker returned to the office to the praises from the others for everyone had been pranked before this day. The plan was now in full swing. The ecstatic group gathered by the slightly ajar office door with boom box in hand cued up watching the elevator for their guest of honor returning from the bank's main lobby. The elevator opened revealing a very red faced humiliated teary-eyed person, with hilarity coming from the portable peanut gallery behind him. Swiftly walking he dropped the crumpled piece of paper from his back that held the mantra:' I like to sniff people's bicycles seats'. Nothing could erase the humor and awe of all the tellers and customers in the lobby that morning. As he approached the office, his co-workers began singing along with Rod Stewart on the boom box 'If you think I'm sexy...'

When you see something funny just know your motivation. Laughter is healthy!

THOUGHT #102

The Ability to Give

'What we give away is what we get to keep.' In other words what we cultivate is what we get to experience. To grasp this idea, one must shift in thinking to the idea of being an avenue of grace, prosperity, and inspiration to the receiver. To some this idea may seem strange or even profane. From a finite perspective anything given is a sacrifice, something lost, something needed to collect interest on because the giver suffered or gave up temporarily. For those who dwell in the secret place of the Most High, giving and receiving are but one act - where lack and fear are wanton strangers.

The hummingbird does its delightful dance pollinating the garden effortlessly all the while enjoying the results of its previous giving. All the color and fragrance it helped create is available to it.

Remember the story of the rabbi who upon returning home one evening found it being robbed. As the thief was running down the garden path, the rabbi chased after him throwing his best sandals towards him saying "Please take these also! I give you these and all that you have!" The rabbi knew the secret of gracious mercy and its constant compensation. When asked to explain his actions. He replied, "I wanted him to feel forgivingness in action. I did not want his actions to be credited to his lack and neediness but rather to his ability to receive and my ability to give."

THOUGHT #103

Can You Measure Your Dream

The Laws of Success are defined by those who make them. Make your own. Just remember the short stick is best suited for small mouth dogs. The bigger the stick, the bigger the dream, the bigger the dog. Play hard, play young and live voraciously for it is Spirit that gives you life and inhabits even your toes. Only pull punches like a grasshopper picks cotton - which it never does. Never measure yourself by another's meter. Learn from him how to measure that is all.

'You are what your deep, driving desire is.

As your desire is, so is your will.

As your will is, so is your deed.

As your deed is, so is your destiny.'

Brihadaranyaka Upanishad IV.4.5

THOUGHT #104

Thoughts of a Mad Man

The thoughts of a mad man

are just that.

They are feeding a

frenzy of lame kite

spin.

Building steam for an engine

with a short run of track. All

the excessive thought without

relief.

What becomes of that mad man

when Pure Consciousness overtakes

him?

From exhaustion he

collapses. All his thinking

knotted and left where it

lies.

The ghosts he created are transformed.

Helpers they become of the Most High.

Incessant waves of Love bathe his wounded soul.

As dirt falls from his face in the mirror of his hands,

and Light shines all about

him, he has but one

thought train 'I am still,

my mind is calm, I feel

peace, here with my God

do I offer my Gratitude,

I am safe...'

THOUGHT #105

To Conquer

Let's face it we have been tired of a lot of things in our own lives. We see people our age and younger seemingly doing well and we say 'how come?' to ourselves. A better question might be 'where do I start?'

We start our change with a twinge of desire, a willingness to shift 3 inches from our current center (that fixed place of perception). We allow ourselves to follow our own unfolding. We are totally OK with all we have committed, all blunders, all the good and not so good, all missed desires. We accept this Gracepoint of soulful awakening, realizing all things were preparatory.

Now the obvious place to start is where we are at. Yes, right now, move over 3 inches. If standing at a window notice the shift in available view. How does that feel? Maybe a little odd! Don't worry we will get used to it and soon we will look for that feeling as an indicator we are evolving in all areas of life. We begin to see change and how it feels to make a shift. This little exercise costs us nothing to experience.

In this life we either play behind the edge of the shadows of our past that preoccupy our present where there is always fading light. OR we follow the sun of enlightenment by readjusting our personal inward stance to capture new vistas and horizons that are constantly being illuminated.

THOUGHT #106

Changing Lanes

We live in a world of change sometimes very swift and other times complex and slow, like brain surgery.

Change can be exhilarating often giving us the impression of defying gravity. Of being able to dissolve all binding ties and the list goes on.

What helps during the 'change' event is timely messages from the Omniverse, texts from unusual friends or acquaintances. You know synchronicity! Divine timing!

Sometimes we get so caught up in the activity of changing that we seem hesitant to actually complete the change. It may seem better to us and for us to simply keep the turning signal on and to ride that lane. To keep participating in change activities and groups yet never quite moving off center and making an actual change, even if just for change sake. People will say they had a revelation, or some profound inspirational episode and after several months they are still wrestling that angel for a blessing. They are still riding the change lane with the blinker on. Let's be mindful that 'change' should reflect an unfolding not an abiding.

THOUGHT #107

Sparks of Change

We excel at so many things often to the decrement of the greater things to accomplish. We can win marathons, yet never outrun the feeling of despise for something our parents may have done or didn't do. We can win the heart of someone we find irresistible only to realize they cannot live up to our expectations or satisfy our inward feeling of loneliness that gnaws at us.

When the avatars and prophets have spoken, the veil that separated us from greater Consciousness was parted. In their wake, religions and great movements were formed. Many came seeking to alleviate all their suffering. Many were told that all their suffering would be over when they died. So, they beat the pillow of their daily experience until that end of their life occurred and then they went on to their 'rewards'. Often when we slow down the pillow beating we find ourselves destitute of any excuses of why our lives are not better before we die. What we find is that we may be experiencing the ghosts of old movies playing out for us and through us. Those ghosts are old tracks of hurts and other junk baggage that become our current views, perspectives and even behaviors. These outcroppings show us a less than ideal family member, co-worker or friend. Consequently, our ideal perception of them is now shattered and we blame them for who we are. The picture only gets clearer as we polish the mirror. As Gandhi stated 'Be the change you wish to see in the world' and Michael sang 'I'm talking to the man in the mirror'.

THOUGHT #108

How Shall We Choose

Ice cream melts at temperatures above itself. Cotton spoils with the weevils. Ants devour the best packed picnic lunch.

In each situation we see a circumstance that indicates a natural order. Each entity in its formed state can be acted upon by another outside itself.

In striking contrast of all species, be they plant, mineral, substance or animal, only humankind has the ability for self-sabotage; to be an active or reactive component in the individual undoing by the individual itself.

We can create one heck of a mess for ourselves or a glorious opposite. Call it self-determinism, free will, or unbounded choice.

But know that this unique position of abilities to create, explore or explode are simply choices of voices. What shall we choose today, a meltdown, spoiled goods, loss or the life of the phoenix?

THOUGHT #109

Rounding to the Next Higher

As I stood along a particular sidewalk on a certain day observing the strength and contrast of a shrubbery bed with rocks as the base, curiosity became me. On this particular moment, I let my eyes ramble over the sea of river rock. It was just like Christmas, to my surprise Santa had left no stone unturned, for there were no jagged edges, all the stones were smooth.

My curiosity would not stop so I extended keen eyes to the nearby dike lining the river and whew! ... every rock was rough and had unfinished edges. Until I made the comparison I could have taught the unenlightened that rocks are found round fresh out of deep ground. Noting this I turned within briefly and internalized this grace-filled moment.

I was most thankful for the anger, disappointment and heart moments to remind me that in this River of Life this is just what is needed to make me smoother and rounder so I too can decorate the Evergreen and let my Light shine. My life still has some unsmooth edges and no doubt yours too. So, the next time you are in a crowd of people, look them over. Then know that some are fresh from the quarry and not shuffled smooth by the ongoing strong streams of Life. When you look at your friend, who do you see?... Someone rounded to the next higher version of themselves?

THOUGHT #110

The Win

When we let old habits die who said we can't celebrate and be Joyous.

For there are at least two things that have happened: We made a change that took courage. We moved to somewhere we had not been. Sometimes the change is made out of desperation. Nonetheless, we should feel a sense of accomplishment for we successfully used the eraser end of the pencil. We eliminated an old line no longer needed in the picture of life we were drawing.

Secondly, we have consciously or not, participated to some degree in our own unfoldment. We have demonstrated the power of choice. We dared to draw a new line in the redesigning of our life.

There are many reasons to let the old habit die. If for no other reason than to say to yourself, "I win!"

Try saying that seven times without getting tongue tied. I WIN! I WIN! I WIN! I WIN! I WIN! I WIN! I WIN!

THOUGHT #111

Paranormal Activity

We heard this term a lot in the 80s and 90s, even into the 2000s. Thanks to X-files and TV ghost stories. Of course, got to love Ghost Busters! Question is, when we go to work don't we think they missed some of those goblins?!

Seriously there are a couple of things that ring contrary to what is typically called paranormal activity. Now we are attempting to rediscover those talents through greater scientific study of what is called psychic phenomena. Telepathy, instantaneous healings, synchronicity of events and fractional slices of time have become more than just colorful coffee bar talk. Even though some popular religious teachings still deny the beneficence or 'normality' of such phenomena, the precise documentation is growing. Telepathy existed before as a belief that God heard our prayers. It stood to reason that if Spirit is Omnipresent, then praying to God was simply an invisible means of communication! Ancient manuscripts speak of a knowing about shifts in events. Am told Marlo Morgan's book, *Mutant Message Down Under*, captures the essence of 'tuning in' on others. The oracles, seers and prophets were considered specialists of acceptable 'normal' activity. Talk with many hypnotists and they will tell you about diseases that disappear from their patients. Again, easily understood as normal activity in their line of work. Reading the research results and experiences of enlightened researchers such as Dr. Masaru Emoto (*Messages from Water*) and Dr. Bruce Lipton (*Biology of Belief*) and Master Chunyi Lin (*Born a Healer*) will awaken the sense that for too long we have lived with confined perceptions. These perceptions have impacted us to the degree we have believed what is hard or taboo is actually normal and effortlessness when working in the realm of Spirit, Light and Energy. Call your friend this afternoon (without your cell phone). You may find it busy but keep trying. Frustration in this activity is expected and *normal* since we have adopted so many *abnormal* paradigms. Feel the hug I just gave you!

THOUGHT #112

Tuning In

The only normal relationship and state of affairs is that which is breathed through us by the Ultimate Spirit as It expresses in our individual consciousness. This comes when we cease being and acting like 'a man whose breath is in his nostrils' as Joel Goldsmith a 20th century mystic would say.

Our normal relationship is how it has always been - despite appearances of any kind. For what could possibly separate one from the Love of God. The crack addict feels the rush of God as their heart continues beating even though that experience is artificially fabricated and dishonoring to the body temple. Let's not discount the 'happy' feeling of Sister Mamie as she turns over the pews during a Sunday morning service while screaming 'Jesus Jesus Jesus!' While these examples may be extreme demonstrations of an ecstatic feeling they are by no means reflective of the full measure of a relationship with God.

Upon awaking we realize that all our needs met. We have slept and arisen unharmed and intact. Thus, gratitude is in order. Not just for the present moment but including every single moment of our lives. Feeling this expanded and deepened sense of Oneness we center ourselves in the full thought that because of who we really are (I AM), we have available resources to meet the requirements of this day.

We have vibrationally attuned our internal dial to one of Realization and true wealth. We realize further there can be no tear in the Fabric of Life, nor any shortcomings in circumstances. Our normal relationship reflects an acceptance and vacating any idea to the contrary of being a branch on the tree or the tree itself, gently and consistently experiencing the depth and height of the Soul's tryst with its Creator.

THOUGHT #113

Jet-skis and Rooster Tails

Speed, wind, engine roar and water are some of the elements that make jet-skiing such a popular hot weather thrill. If you notice there are two natural elements making the exhilaration.

Fresh air for one is filled with healthy Qi (chee) that promotes and enables activity! Although when unbalanced, can be what we term 'destructive'. 'The ancient Chinese art of practical ecology is called

Feng Shui or 'Wind Water'. One can balance the flow of Qi in their environment by following wind water concepts. Water contains our genealogical aspects, our bodies and represents that which is passed from generation to generation. Water represents the primal '*budding*' force of human nature. It is also the realm of collective and personal unconscious. The Archetype for water is the 'Philosopher'. The Philosopher searches doggedly for truth. All the while searching for meaning that transcends the rudderless meandering of human affairs.

The question is, are all the jet-skiers really philosophers or are they just skimming the surface of our collective unconscious?

THOUGHT #114

Who is Hurting Who

When we say we have suffered enough, do we really mean it? Or do we mean that what is offending us or hurting us has become bound to our conscious mind. And are we keeping it as emotional baggage to leverage our fires of resentment and anger for something that was over so five seconds ago. If the idea of suffering is in the 'hands' of the perceiver, then shouldn't the pain go away when we decide?

Often, we are tempted to linger with the pain long after the source of the offence is removed. A prolonged feeling of pain also causes us to form twisted ideas about others. We begin to project on the new people in our lives such that they remind us of our past. We must move from ideological concept of 'victim'. Every dog is not the one that bit us when were 3 years old unless we have not moved psychologically or emotionally from that scene. To continue to hold others accountable for how we feel is not taking any power from them. Instead it holds us powerless and we continue to 'suffer' even though the original source of the hurt is long gone.

When the hurt feeling arises take notice who is doing it ... the new boyfriend or your idea of the new boyfriend wrapped in your dad's vibration. Choose today whom you will serve, a victim mentality that keeps you ill at ease or a sense of Infinite Being. One who recognizes their Divinity! Turn in your badge and walk free for you are neither the sheriff nor the jailed!

THOUGHT #115

What Comes Next

We would be remiss to not give gratitude for the butterfly showing us there is life after life. Its brightly colored 4-inch wings flipping erotically and erratically upon the lavender crests of tall flowers. The tail part of the wing is painted a solid blue that matches the sky.

Now we know she was not born that way the First time, yet her splendor has always been there. Mixed in its heritage are the trees, soil, wind, rain, and willingness. The forgoing elements prove inseparable to the butterfly. Without a tree to nurture and feed the First Life the Second Life does not come. Without the wind and rain the seed of the tree would not become. The soil is mother to the flowers used in the Second Life. Thus, we learn about 'inter-being' from our friend who is not separate from us. Its willingness to transform is a call we all must heed now or at some greater point in time.

As we surge in the rediscovery of our True Nature, we stress less from seeming difficulties. We take comfort that surely as we 'inter-are', Life will continually support us from, to and through and beyond, the First Life. That Life leads to the Second Life each second, each moment our heart turns its attention to the greater calling of Light that pulls us towards our Complete Beingness, not the strains that seem to drive us to change. Death of one situation or 'mini-life' does not have God gasping or the heavens toiling to see what will happen. For God Itself is the very metamorphosizing activity. So, when we look into the water puddle and behold ourselves, let us softly speak 'we know what comes next'!

THOUGHT #116

Liberation Consciousness

'I came that you might have life abundantly' is how one Avatar put it. Once we begin to dance with the Eternal I AM Presence the fruits and the sweat from that dance is a vitality that grows beyond the material dimension.

One's deepest yearnings often default to having a sense of freedom – be it a simple freedom from a nagging ache. Yet the deeper snag on their soul lingers. This nagging feeling has led to many selfless acts of courage and inventions.

Our higher Self recognizes the better life from Its Infinite vantage point. Those of us open to Its Voice will seek that better way. First shattering the old paradigm within our own lives thus removing the mote we projected onto our brother. We must gain fresh vision for ourselves if we are to come into full realization of that I AM consciousness. Once we begin to taste the fruits of this marriage – our heart with Its Creator, the higher Self expands that freedom into our experience. The result is our activity no longer is governed by a belief in two powers hence the bonds of Doubt and Fear play no significant role to the point that we breathe more fully of the Power and Ever Presence of the Almighty. Our song is gratitude and we speak of Oneness! Every great one has been liberated first in their own consciousness then reached out to those who had ears to hear the Idea of One God unified. This carried them beyond human and spiritual slavery. They were able to face Pilate and acknowledge only One Power. Be liberated this day by knowing that No Thing can separate you from the Love of God and God is LOVE! There is No Thing else.

THOUGHT #117

Jigsaw Talk

We solve the jigsaw puzzle a piece at a time. There is a simple lesson here. We group like pieces together. We put the border together. Then assemble the familiar pictured scenes. Next begins the hunt for the right shape and openings. Here we use a lot of intuitive hunches, visual dexterity or a lot a hand movement.

Could this be a better method of moving forward with the flow of Life, ours in particular? First getting a vision of what that desired life feels like; looks like, etc. Assemble all the known elements. Framing that vision with what essentials will make the borders. For example, if it is to experience living in a tropical place but leaving your current country is out, then you have a border piece. Now mind you not all our jigsaw visions will have border pieces initially. This is okay. Now comes the really fun part! The hunt for clues prevails as we are rejuvenated with each piece that falls into place. Those pieces could be information, encouragement from a stranger, foreclosure, job relocation and literally almost anything since we know that Life is inclusive without coincidences. Synchronicity and intuition guide us through inserting the pieces of deep emotional releases and conscious shifts in our hearts into the right perspectives that allow us to see our vision more clearly. Sometimes we may have assembled large sections of our future life together yet finding they do not connect with the border because we have that section turned upside down. The friend we're trying to make a part of our dream has a dream of their own and is making one with their new partner. So, their role becomes less of a fitting piece, requiring us to reorient the remaining pieces we find. However, the beauty of the nature of the jigsaw puzzle is that one piece can be left aside while the remaining image evolves. Our vision of what is to be pulls us and the more we view the vision the more we want to complete it, so we stay engaged and active in a progressive manner. The calamities of the past are not so much the fuel that drives us forward as are the 'Preferences' we desire that call to us. The fearful man running from a bear with no future vision of what safety looks like in his mind may run only deeper into the woods and find no relief or find another bear. Step proudly into the next grander version of yourself! Solve your own puzzle.

THOUGHT #118

The Law of Expectancy

If we were all expected to leap the same height some of us would be left out. If we were all expected to prepare really good healthy meals, some of us would starve. Thank you God for not asking that of us! Have we asked ourselves who is making up these rules of expectation that have little eternal value? Will we become our likeness in purgatory for not observing birthdays or other special days? *A Course in Miracles* discusses the energy put forth to cultivate 'specialness'. Specialness can be a sand trap for us if we let ego rule the day. The ego wants praise of separaticity not because it is linked with something of transcendent value. For instance, birthdays are special fun days and even more so when we realize there is an inherent sacredness there. We are in fact honoring those persons for bringing forth a quality of God in a unique fashion. We are appreciating the blessing and the blessedness of that person as a vessel thru which the Light Itself shines. So, reflect back on this moment when you are invited to the next special occasion. We are here to bear eternal gifts of incredible value to each other. So sacred and timely they cannot be bought but only given as received. If you need a place to start think hugs and smiles for miles. Treat every interaction as a Holy Instant. Expect it!

THOUGHT #119

Independent Thinking

I love the independent thinker concept. I tried that with math when in grade school. Even though I arrived at the correct answer my methodology was different so I was told I did it 'wrong'. Even now I question whether society is really open to independent thinkers for they seem to be everywhere. They are the real leaders and shapers of the future society. Some of us succumb to peer mediocrititis. For you grown folks that is inflammation of peer opinion. Those not succumbing will admire the independent thinkers for their reliance on different methods to arrive at right answers. We will come to admire their sanctified life.

THOUGHT #120

The True State

The true state of independence lies in the degree of freedom from the finite and a giving of one's self over to limitless Consciousness. In that state what is truly valuable comes forth and new plateaus of Being emerge.

THOUGHT #121

Close Enough

They met

They walked

They stared

They talked

They glanced as if eyes could speak

They glided down the path

To hold hands …too weak.

One dreamt of the great first kiss;

The Other dreamt of one they would always miss.

They met

They walked more

They shared stories

They were not sure

They each held breath

They each held back

Each felt they were close enough.

THOUGHT #122

The Changewinds

Because we have changed (whether you noticed or not- ignorance being no excuse!), we can never truly go home. We go there and nothing but everything seems to have changed. We see others differently. Now this is not always a physical circumstance.

Changewinds move all things. Even trash is blown by the wind till it finds a catching point. It is on those days in our lives when the winds of change seem to be blowing extra hard, we may opt to hang out where the trash is collecting, out of the way of changewinds. These are the places where the air is stale, short on vitality and offer little circulation or growth. In spite of those qualities, some may find comfort. Familiar territory on the mental level, not necessarily a physical place.

For we who are seeking that grander version of ourselves and in others we recognize this trash collecting place at best a temporary shelter, a momentary lapse of judgment, a place to catch our breath but not to grow roots. Those trash collecting places are not always physical!

With a flash of gratitude, we remember THAT which pulled us out into the Changewind in the first place. What were we seeking? Where were we headed? We ask these questions momentarily. When we accept our soul's response to the questions we reach inwardly to our heart and know that this is how we see others different from our past. We see in Love.

Thanks, Jodee K.

THOUGHT #123

Forming a More Perfect Union

There are times when we wake up and realize that how the world was when we went to sleep is now somehow different and we must live with the changes. To do so requires living from an intentionality of wanting to form a more perfect union.

To create a more perfect union means right alignment. As the nut on a bolt. When the external threads of the bolt are rightly fit with the corresponding internal threads of the nut a more perfect union comes. There is harmony and strength in that relationship. This has universal application for all that exists is part of a relationship. Those who do not have an affirmative one with their vehicles may experience 'loss of control' or have situations develop from lack of maintenance.

Am I forming a more perfect union with the life I desire to live? This is the question of the day.

THOUGHT #124

Loving Yourself

'The greatest love of all is learning how to love yourself'. Listen to that song at least 21 times then you will find a reason to start the romance all over again. Like you did when you first arrived on this planet. Nobody can love you like you can.

THOUGHT #125

God's Got this

There is a place to go when things are hectic and seem out of control. This place will free us from any doubt, worry and even pain. No, I am not talking about some distant heaven after we "die". Though I am talking from a place with no geographic point, it is actually quite near and 'at hand'. It is simple and yet fundamental to our spiritual and emotional equilibrium. We hear and read the sages, prophets and Rumi speak of peace with ecstasy and agree with head nods and question marks on our brow. How can that be we ask? Even though we live in a dimension of propagated duality, the Law of Life is singular. Of a truth is if your vision is single, then your whole body and body of affairs will be filled with light. Today we reach or rather LET that Law of Life do its thing. We rest in knowing that 'stuff' worked itself out before we got here; many times, before; and will continue. That is the beauty of the nomena called Eternity and Infinity. Simply put... God's got this!

THOUGHT #126

Loving

There is nothing like being here for yourself! Love is the first quality of lasting substance. Yet some do not get it. They feel it is too easy or too hard. Then there are those of us who get it. We are kind to ourselves. We show love to ourselves at which point we can begin the journey outside of our hearts into that of another. What occurs after that is breathtaking and mind-blowing. We become more our true selves when Love lives through us.

THOUGHT #127

Learning to Love

There are many ways the masters and ancient ones have shared with us to develop compassion. Probably the most amazing and yet least understood or appreciated is to use our momentary feelings, be they sadness or desire or some other, to learn what it feels like. Simply learn it... how the tear forms, or throat tightens and all the accompanying, underlying nuances and how they can affect our conversations, our levels of happiness. Then use the learning of it to begin to love yourself more appropriately, realizing that what we are experiencing is just shaping a tool we will use to lift others as we move through life. This expands the capacity for compassion. We find those feelings are not our condemnation or story but will increase our understanding of others. Ultimately allowing us to love more sincerely, deeply and assuredly unconditionally.

THOUGHT #128

Beyond the Limit

If we have any limits it is because we see them. What is beyond current limits is Infinite. The weight lifter adding just 5 pounds to the bar and performing a full bench press of 305 pounds will have passed the previous 'limit' of a 300-pound press. Whatever we do beyond our current observed limit places us that much further into the Infinite. Live On!

THOUGHT #129

Unmaking God

It stands to reason if there be but one Life Giver and that is the Source of All life and the very activity back of all life, then the resulting conclusion is that all activity from the subtle to the gross, must have as its sponsoring energy that which is Whole, Perfect and Infinite – Life Giving and Life Sustaining. That being said let us return no more to eat of the tree that causes death through stagnation and retardation – that tree of judgment of what is good or evil. The One Life Giver cannot give forth both bitter and sweet. For to one man what is bitter is sweet to another. Let us this day unmake God in our image and simply confess we do not know nor understand. Let us further confess that in our ignorance we have squandered our ability of thinking consciously and now are undone by where we are at spiritually, mentally and physically. We left, and are right now willing to return home to the Kingdom within, the place of the Life Giver and Sustainer, our Father's House to be judged not, but embraced!

THOUGHT #130

Set a Goal to Enjoy

Deep gratitude to all who have labored with me this summer season. Another chapter in my life has closed with the passing of my mother in June and having her memorial service last Saturday the day before her 83rd birthday. We celebrated her life spent educating and cultivating the goodness in ourselves and others. My mother shared with me this quote years ago that I carry with me even now: SET A GOAL TO ENJOY THE THINGS YOU DO! IF YOU MEET THIS GOAL EVERY SECOND AND, IN EVERY SITUATION, YOU WILL BE LIVING NOT JUST EXISTING.

THOUGHT #131

Be a First-Class Passenger

For those looking for the Universe to fix their life, remember you must become a passenger. You are not driving so keep your hands off the wheel. You are being driven to take a course of action. Yet also realize that the present circumstances are a clear representation of the Divinely stated principle "according to your faith, be it done unto you". No contradiction here. It is based on Divine Law. There is an Intelligence that is above and beyond what we can fathom. It is leading us to a perfect outworking where the victory; the rebalancing; the salvation; the correction is at hand. We can't see it because we are too short to see over the steering wheel. Relax the grip and breathe knowing God's got this. Our best seat is as a First-Class passenger. Where is pure unadulterated, unconditional love taking you?

THOUGHT #132

Falling in Love

Subsequent to falling in love is discovery. Subsequent to discovery is recovery. Not necessarily recovery as if from a bad fall but just adjusting our balance to new territory

– Coz Ruthles

THOUGHT #133

Not Timid

We ponder about intimidation. We might often think of a world with a crisis of intimidation. The structure of the word itself is a clue of what is actually being called forth - the state of not timid. Sometimes we do not recognize ourselves when we are 'out of character'. We resolve to respond not so timidly. Sometimes people, places and things can intimidate. Yet it is entirely a subjective matter. A perceiver is the receiver becoming the believer in the 'intimidating' circumstances. In other words, we see it, we label it so and we buy into it. Sometimes so much that clarity of inspired thinking and feeling is miles away in the bottom of a boat. There is an enlightening story on the rules of intimidation found in the first book of Samuel Chapter 14. In short, the young men heeded the call not be timid. Know this day, even this moment that God, the Law of Life is with you according to your heart.

THOUGHT #134

Seek the Eternal Vantage Point

'Forget about your life situation for a while and pay attention to your life. Your life situation exists in time. Your life is now. Your life situation is mind-stuff. Your life is real.' Eckhart Tolle

Eckhart seems to say touch the very present. That split second before you speak to your child or spouse or partner or blow the kiss. Become aware of your breathing, the tension or heart feeling. As you begin to notice these sorts of things also notice that cannot be you for you are the one observing those things. As you begin to work this into the fabric of conscious life you will find that you are just observing life situations. Life becomes that eternal vantage point of the observer.

So how ya livin' now?

THOUGHT #135

Hidden Power to Become a Beneficial Presence

The power of the mushroom is in its ability to grow in the dark. Compare this to human nature and its ability to move from its history.

THOUGHT #136

Desire

Out of necessity a delicacy is born. What is your 'desire' or rather what is it you want to see 'from the Father'. Every delicacy is derived from a basic need and will satisfy still only that basic need no matter how well it is presented. This should not stop any of us from trying to look and do our best. De-Sire is from the Father and by the Father.

THOUGHT #137

Learning To Be How To Be

A leaf knows of peace. Learn from it!

THOUGHT #138

Self-Watering

Forgiveness brings us to the present time. Many who don't forgive feel they have something to lose or something has been lost. Those are usually the ones who are clinging to ideas of limited substance and disconnectedness with their Divine heritage.

As we move towards having the heart of God, Infinite Spirit will reveal to us a path to undo the congestion in our heart. Infinite Spirit will reveal to us a path to undo the congestion in our heart.

It does not necessarily expect us to fix a situation which is what many of us fear. Rather It seeks to comfort us as spoken in the 23rd Psalm. It does the work from a Higher Dimension than from the lower state of mind that caused our dilemma or our feelings about it. Take heart that God is still in charge.

Live in Love with the Divine. Read the works of Rumi.

We all have food we know not of, buried within. Those talents if you will, are dislodged and refreshed by the degree of Eternal living waters we allow to flow forth. In other words, our connectedness to Spirit becomes our Self-watering and Self-blossoming.

Hallelujah!

THOUGHT #139

Have a Better Day

"The past is over. It can touch me not"... A Course in Miracles

We cannot undo what has been done yet we offer grace as we have been shown how to live better. More love more wealth. More health. Deeper, truer forgiveness. Yes grace. That we live better today than yesterday. Heart open. Mind still. Body, a willing instrument through which the Divine can express Its Will more clearly.

There is someone somewhere who is willing to accept your grace today as it has been given to you. Do you accept this soulful opportunity?

THOUGHT #140

Sound of the Genuine

"Whatever may be the tensions and the stresses of a particular day, there is always lurking close at hand the trailing beauty of forgotten joy or unremembered peace."

— Howard Thurman, Meditations of the Heart

If I have learned anything this week is that constantly returning to mindfulness practice is salvation. That practice keeps us from the clutches of a reptilian, ego-based Halloween life.

For me that mindfulness comes from chanting 'Divine Love is doing Its perfect work in and thru me now '. Followed by 'Divine Love is doing Its perfect work in and thru 'whatever, fill in the blank' now'. 'Divine Love heals, Divine Love seals, Divine Love reveals, Divine Love fills, Divine Love thrills, Divine Love creates right adjustment in my life now and all is well'. You will find as you do these statements of mindfulness many other thoughts will come in. Don't refuse them just let them enter and keep going. Spirit has a way of working Its way in. I have had an even bigger blessing since I started doing this intensively in September by inserting my feelings about a situation, person and even myself. Like 'Divine Love is doing Its perfect work in and thru my feelings about wealth right now'.

You can practice in a mirror. First notice your face, the brow lines, eyes and cheeks then close your eyes and repeat the Divine Love statements several times. Relax, expect nothing while doing this. Then open your eyes and look at your face.

How do you feel? How does your face look?

"There is something in every one of you that waits and listens for the sound of the genuine in yourself. It is the only true guide you will ever have. And if you cannot hear it, you will all of your life spend your days on the ends of strings that somebody else pulls."

— Howard Thurman

THOUGHT #141

Expansion by Default or Intention

When we wander we do not wander far from our level of the thoughts of our understanding.

In one of my seminary classes the instructor asked the profound question: 'How did the sheep get lost in the first place?'

The sheep was feeding its interests. Obviously, we are not sheep, but we will nibble as far as our tastes are satisfied. The desire to fly by plane was a nibble now we wander into deeper space with our eyes on Mars. The premise is we can't go anywhere or discover new territory unless we rise above our current level of thinking. Although we sometimes just wander into varied states of lostness.

Though there is a deeper thirst and hunger that nibbles at us: want of mate, money, power, fame, and even a wholly peaceful mind. We find that a recommitment to Self is necessary. That is the real journey and reward of our wandering through life. Seek and gain the All then all else will be added. A Unity saying I learned years ago is *a thought held in mind produces after its own kind*.

How does your life reflect this? Is it taking you towards a place of peace?

THOUGHT #142

Divine Confidence

A blind snack shop owner was told by one of his morning customers there were only three small cartons of milk left in the cooler. The physically blind owner busy doing other morning preparations paused for a moment then responded to the customer, "well the milkman is supposed to come today, if he doesn't God better send a cow." Then he resumed his activity unbothered.

What a prosperous faith. Certainly not by sight, but he had a matter of fact confidence in Divine deliverance. Can we anchor ourselves in such a relaxed acceptance of Hearing the Inaudible, Seeing the Invisible and Feeling the Intangible Presence? Let us have the Divine Confidence of the blind man.

THOUGHT #143

Resting in Peace

Life's circumstances challenge our understanding of it. Yet once having tasted the liberating thought of our life being an expression of the Infinite we rest in peace. We rest into our feeling nature that we are one with that Life and we are abiding with each other in that Truth.

THOUGHT #144

From Satisfaction to Embellishment

Sometimes just a fraction of circumstance has filled and fulfilled. Level to the top of the glass is satisfaction to some. The nectar once tasted seems so right we embark on a journey to dispel the fog of our itch. Seeking more, more often. We see the thing clearly, judge it meaningful and to be had. We grow towards what is satisfying.

Being satisfied; living in satisfaction gives way to the behavior of showing it. We cannot hide it. It may be in some sort of subtle way or could be flamboyant. For when we share we feel compelled to use adjectives, adverbs or exaggerate. Not necessarily because we want to aggrandize but because it feels so good that our satisfaction has reached a limit that is pressing us to overflow.

THOUGHT #145

Divine Cloth

Only what is built with eternal fabric can last for it uses nothing that could be captured by time. Your test for today is to see how many of those transcending fibers or qualities you use. As you get good at this it will become what the world may call 'second nature'. Actually, in Reality this ability is your 'first nature'. We are made by the Eternal Infinite. Those are the dynamic Divine genes we have.

THOUGHT #146

The Pearl

If you think living the big life is existing in an oyster shell, then just know and accept the fact that all the sand coming your way is so you can produce something of beauty not for yourself. We are called to lives of excellence and outshining. The Pearl results from what we do with our lives that gives value to Life. Selah.

THOUGHT #147

The Great Inaudible

Deep listening goes beyond the audible. That is when Spirit can be heard. What we should take away from the sacred altar of meditation is an attitude of how to be more generous with Love.

Not our petty form or idea of love. Beyond sympathy or empathy therein lies the unfathomable well of compassion.

THOUGHT #148

Recognition in Resurrection

The power of resurrection is found in no particular person, no particular cell or doctrine. That Power of Life and its corresponding activity of regeneration is beyond human intellectual intent or detection. Its takes soulful openness to recognize the domain of Father-Mother God. When we recognize our awakening to this Presence and Power we will find we can accept a new understanding that places us spiritually in the Garden of Eden where all needs are met.

THOUGHT #149

Being Who We Are

The principle or nature of the ripple is not to grow itself that happens by what it is.

THOUGHT #150

Peace That is God

If we ever needed the Peace that is God it is now. When we have occasion to be anxious for everything let us not forsake the moments of quiet, of a thoughtful hug, an intentional smile, a simple agape love-filled glance. Let us not miss this right now moment to remember grandparents, the newly birthed, the citizen in a physically war-torn country and the one with a war in their mind. When we remember let us remember that the thread of Life runs through all, often having its greatest impact perhaps when our friends appear to be suffering. These are the moments we open wide for an even bigger experience of the Peace that is God. We know that Life is Holy and its presence touches all right now. Spilling its compassion, its delight, its restorative, regenerative power and intelligence over whatever the situation is at hand. If we embrace but one bit of defining wisdom right now it is the healing of our minds so that our thinking is transformed to see God at work. Amen. Aho. Namaste!

THOUGHT #151

Gratitude Cascade

Just for the season try speaking one line of gratitude every minute. Another thought will show up and then another. Before you know it the once forgotten names, possibly of your elementary school teachers will come across your lips and after about an hour you will be exhausted. Yes, what a list of things we can be thankful for.

THOUGHT #152

Stirring Vision

Without vision they perish.

Without a dream they clamor but for little.

With sleep they do little more than breathe.

For sleep is given to the masses; masses yearning for dim light, not vision.

Oh, but the dream can carry them away and dispel the repression a little while...

the dream comforts a mind in shambles or stupor...yet means little when the body's eyes are opened to believing a lesser perspective...less than full Life expression and true possibility... But for the Power of Vision... for the mind that is touched by Soul begins its leap, its rage of burn. It grasps the tail of a freeing dream showing a new birth of liberty.

That mind casts the bright shadow of a forward path; seizing fragments and pigments to color it in.

No more letting sleep dull the waking hours. For the Soul is heard, not weeping but firm and convinced. It spreads its desires like a tender blanket before lovers. It sweetly oozes words to make clear the fresh picture. It breathes across the conscious, the intellect, and the false and deceived perceptive feelings to fan the young flames of a better day.

This transpiration occurs to the being that is no longer asleep in their walking, but deeply inhaling that dream like the breath that is God.

We rest in peace because a vision is shared and affirmed…

We wrestle and quarrel not nor strive for naught because we now know the Will, the plans It has dreamed for us. We live as happily as the path of the butterfly.

Let gratitude be the sole of your foot… touching… touching… touching… everywhere you go.

Happy Thanks and Giving to all…

THOUGHT #153

Are We Connected

On the unseen level our souls find ways to make the connection. When you can't seem to find a way to connect allow your vision to see deeper into faith that the Everlasting is working it out.

Remember it was Friday but Sunday came too. It is all about having a resurrection attitude.

Enjoy the season!

THOUGHT #154

Undefined Emergence

The child is not mine is a truth. Michael Jackson sang it. Joseph husband of St. Mary said it.

Eyes have not seen; ears have not heard what the I AM has in store for you an ancient mystic declared. "I know the plans I have for you, to prosper you" were the words given to another prophet of old. From Robert Browning's much heralded work *Paracelsus,* we are advised to *release the inner splendor.*

We do not know the full potential of any Idea that comes through us. This is the greater phenomenon of birthing. We are simply opening out a way for something new to come by way of us. We don't own the life that is generating itself within us. The I AM, Infinite and Eternal Presence is the only real Life–Giver or Source. The child is not ours. It is us! Neither gold in hand or land came from us. We can choose what to do with it but we did not create it. It is with great presence of a humble heart that we bow down our egos to realize that there is Something Good moving at all times in all places preparing a way and a place for Itself. Let us birth wisely and be One with It.

THOUGHT #155

Daily Response

Birthing implies an expected outcome. Much like the singer Sade sings…*'every day is Christmas and every night is New Year's Eve.'* Embracing this concept means each day becomes one of birthing. We begin seeing the new and fresh all the time. It implies living from a place of positive expectancy. Not worrying as prayers to the devil as Bob Marley called it. Instead getting a feeling of how great it will be to open the day by tearing the ribbons off and unfolding gratitude that all needs are met. Giving thanks the Mother of Lights knows what good gifts to give. We open out a way for good to come. We let go of what the wrapping should look like, how it should be and simply pay attention to our role in the process of the birthing, the unwrapping. We allow that which is Infinite and Eternal to more fully express Itself. Make your holiday a Holy Day every day and celebrate the new and fresh that is coming to you, through you, as you.

Merry Christmas and bless someone today even if it is yourself.

THOUGHT #156

The Advent of You

Celebrate consciously that every day is an opportunity to unwrap that gift of life. Second by second life moves on. All the shame and ideas of having to live a life from the perspective of a lowly birth or not enoughness has no more credibility in your personal emotional account. ALL TRANSACTIONS YOU HAVE HERETOFORE USED TO BUILD YOUR LIFE – YES, THOSE UNPRODUCTIVE BELIEFS THAT GIVE YOU REASON FOR DOUBT... ARE CANCELLED! THERE IS A NEW YOU BORN THIS MINUTE. SO, WHAT WILL YOU BE TODAY ???

THERE IS SO MUCH LOVE OUT HERE, SO COME ON IN THE WATER IS FINE... TRUST LIFE FOR IT WAS HAPPENING BEFORE YOU ARRIVED!

THOUGHT #159

Four Pillars of Belief

4 things every real believer must have: a belief in some Cosmic connection; a vision of what they expect; a willingness to have something change; and an understanding of what is not required of them.

A real believer anchors himself or herself in a feeling of assured Omnipresence, Omniscience and Omnipotence. They have a belief in something larger than themselves and yet feel a part of It. We are offspring of the Infinite. We can never undo that. The real believer has to have a concept of the outcome they want. Martin Luther King Jr. had a dream that compelled him to expend his life energies in pursuit of it. While our beliefs may not seem as magnificent they are nonetheless just as valid. While we are praying for something, do we expect it to really change? Often the change that is required is from us. This in itself can be both threatening to our self-identification and yet the breakpoint between a real believer and the spiritually young. The fourth element is a revealer of our level of Cosmic consciousness. While we believe something do we feel we have to play the star role and every position? Real believers know that the right people, right circumstances, right adjustments are happening now. The whole idea of believing brings in unknown features. That is why it is important for us to stay tuned in to Supreme Intelligence as we go on believing. Our role may change or consist of simply holding the vision while allowing others to develop and grow.

As we move into this New Year, continue to cultivate Cosmic consciousness that encourages real belief.

Aho`

THOUGHT #160

The Whispers of Seeds

The seed whispers to the earth, let me bury myself in your womb of rich intelligence; let me feel your dark enthusiasm surround me. Let your enriching substance tenderize me and grow me. Cover me, protect me, for change only you can cause. I am a seed in our hands and prosper by your warm breath. My abundance comes from once having lain asleep in you. I flower and bear fruit rising first out of your goodness. I am forever grateful to you for nurturing such a one as I. Yet am I deeply rooted in you, still feeling your pulse of magnificence within me.

THOUGHT #161

What Am I Birthing?

What we have experienced up to now and right now is to a great degree generated by our level of consciousness. We have birthed some joys, some wacky relationships with seemingly weird people. We have even birthed some inspiring critical health and material circumstances; and no doubt some well fabricated illusions about ourselves, others and this 3-D world.

The Bible character Job confessed an undervalued Truth statement when he said what he *feared* the most had come to pass.

Now for those of us who have been studying the Law of Attraction in depth recognize this as a teaching-learning point. We get what we think about most of the time. Be it based on fear or love.

Can we be square shooters and fair witnesses about our lives today? Can we accept the responsibility as beings made in the image and likeness of the Infinite All Powerful, Ever Knowing Presence? Feeling and knowing this we can begin to allow changes to the circumstances our lives are reflecting.

When we find manure in our lives just know there must be a pony or an awfully big toad. Happy New Year's Eve – every night! Thank you, Sade.

NOTES

About the Author

The author was born into a practicing Baptist household but moved into energy work and metaphysical teachings by the time he was a teenager. He credits his natural mother for opening the door to soul expanding opportunities and encouraging his spiritual journey.

He holds a religious teaching certificate from the American Baptist Theological Seminary and a Bachelors of Science in Metaphysical Studies from the International Metaphysical Ministry through the University of Sedona. He is an ordained metaphysical minister residing in the Detroit, Michigan area from where he shares mystical concepts thru scheduled speaking engagements and online content. He can be reached online via info@bepositiveministries.com

Printed in the United States
By Bookmasters